MW01252321

Llewellyn's

Witches' Datebook

2008

Featuring

Art by Jennifer Hewitson

Text by Elizabeth Barrette, Dallas Jennifer Cobb,
Ellen Dugan, Gerina Dunwich, Emely Flak,
Magenta Griffith, Diana Rajchel, Laurel Reufner,
K. D. Spitzer, and Abby Willowroot

ISBN 978-0-7387-0556-9

2008

JANUARY
```
S  M  T  W  T  F  S
         1  2  3  4  5
 6  7  8  9 10 11 12
13 14 15 16 17 18 19
20 21 22 23 24 25 26
27 28 29 30 31
```

FEBRUARY
```
S  M  T  W  T  F  S
                  1  2
 3  4  5  6  7  8  9
10 11 12 13 14 15 16
17 18 19 20 21 22 23
24 25 26 27 28 29
```

MARCH
```
S  M  T  W  T  F  S
                     1
 2  3  4  5  6  7  8
 9 10 11 12 13 14 15
16 17 18 19 20 21 22
23 24 25 26 27 28 29
30 31
```

APRIL
```
S  M  T  W  T  F  S
         1  2  3  4  5
 6  7  8  9 10 11 12
13 14 15 16 17 18 19
20 21 22 23 24 25 26
27 28 29 30
```

MAY
```
S  M  T  W  T  F  S
               1  2  3
 4  5  6  7  8  9 10
11 12 13 14 15 16 17
18 19 20 21 22 23 24
25 26 27 28 29 30 31
```

JUNE
```
S  M  T  W  T  F  S
 1  2  3  4  5  6  7
 8  9 10 11 12 13 14
15 16 17 18 19 20 21
22 23 24 25 26 27 28
29 30
```

JULY
```
S  M  T  W  T  F  S
         1  2  3  4  5
 6  7  8  9 10 11 12
13 14 15 16 17 18 19
20 21 22 23 24 25 26
27 28 29 30 31
```

AUGUST
```
S  M  T  W  T  F  S
                  1  2
 3  4  5  6  7  8  9
10 11 12 13 14 15 16
17 18 19 20 21 22 23
24 25 26 27 28 29 30
31
```

SEPTEMBER
```
S  M  T  W  T  F  S
 1  2  3  4  5  6
 7  8  9 10 11 12 13
14 15 16 17 18 19 20
21 22 23 24 25 26 27
28 29 30
```

OCTOBER
```
S  M  T  W  T  F  S
            1  2  3  4
 5  6  7  8  9 10 11
12 13 14 15 16 17 18
19 20 21 22 23 24 25
26 27 28 29 30 31
```

NOVEMBER
```
S  M  T  W  T  F  S
                     1
 2  3  4  5  6  7  8
 9 10 11 12 13 14 15
16 17 18 19 20 21 22
23 24 25 26 27 28 29
30
```

DECEMBER
```
S  M  T  W  T  F  S
    1  2  3  4  5  6
 7  8  9 10 11 12 13
14 15 16 17 18 19 20
21 22 23 24 25 26 27
28 29 30 31
```

2009

JANUARY
```
S  M  T  W  T  F  S
               1  2  3
 4  5  6  7  8  9 10
11 12 13 14 15 16 17
18 19 20 21 22 23 24
25 26 27 28 29 30 31
```

FEBRUARY
```
S  M  T  W  T  F  S
 1  2  3  4  5  6  7
 8  9 10 11 12 13 14
15 16 17 18 19 20 21
22 23 24 25 26 27 28
```

MARCH
```
S  M  T  W  T  F  S
 1  2  3  4  5  6  7
 8  9 10 11 12 13 14
15 16 17 18 19 20 21
22 23 24 25 26 27 28
29 30 31
```

APRIL
```
S  M  T  W  T  F  S
            1  2  3  4
 5  6  7  8  9 10 11
12 13 14 15 16 17 18
19 20 21 22 23 24 25
26 27 28 29 30
```

MAY
```
S  M  T  W  T  F  S
                  1  2
 3  4  5  6  7  8  9
10 11 12 13 14 15 16
17 18 19 20 21 22 23
24 25 26 27 28 29 30
31
```

JUNE
```
S  M  T  W  T  F  S
    1  2  3  4  5  6
 7  8  9 10 11 12 13
14 15 16 17 18 19 20
21 22 23 24 25 26 27
28 29 30
```

JULY
```
S  M  T  W  T  F  S
            1  2  3  4
 5  6  7  8  9 10 11
12 13 14 15 16 17 18
19 20 21 22 23 24 25
26 27 28 29 30 31
```

AUGUST
```
S  M  T  W  T  F  S
                     1
 2  3  4  5  6  7  8
 9 10 11 12 13 14 15
16 17 18 19 20 21 22
23 24 25 26 27 28 29
30 31
```

SEPTEMBER
```
S  M  T  W  T  F  S
         1  2  3  4  5
 6  7  8  9 10 11 12
13 14 15 16 17 18 19
20 21 22 23 24 25 26
27 28 29 30
```

OCTOBER
```
S  M  T  W  T  F  S
                  1  2  3
 4  5  6  7  8  9 10
11 12 13 14 15 16 17
18 19 20 21 22 23 24
25 26 27 28 29 30 31
```

NOVEMBER
```
S  M  T  W  T  F  S
 1  2  3  4  5  6  7
 8  9 10 11 12 13 14
15 16 17 18 19 20 21
22 23 24 25 26 27 28
29 30
```

DECEMBER
```
S  M  T  W  T  F  S
         1  2  3  4  5
 6  7  8  9 10 11 12
13 14 15 16 17 18 19
20 21 22 23 24 25 26
27 28 29 30 31
```

Editing/design by Ed Day

Cover illustration and interior art © 2007 by Jennifer Hewitson

Art on chapter openings © 2006 by Jennifer Hewitson

Cover design by Anne Marie Garrison

Art direction by Lynne Menturweck

Table of Contents

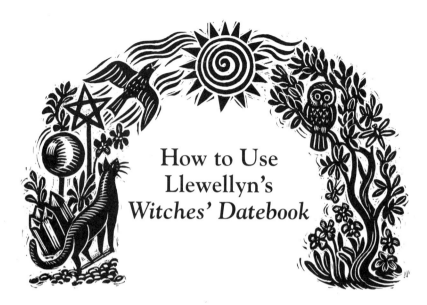

How to Use Llewellyn's Witches' Datebook

W elcome to Llewellyn's *Witches' Datebook 2008*! This datebook was designed especially for Witches, Pagans, and magical people. Use it to plan sabbat celebrations, magic, Full Moon rites, and even dentist and doctor appointments. At right is a symbol key to some of the features of this datebook.

MOON QUARTERS: The Moon's cycle is divided into four quarters, which are noted in the calendar pages along with their exact times. When the Moon changes quarter, both quarters are listed, as well as the time of the change. In addition, a symbol for the new quarter is placed where the numeral for the date usually appears.

MOON IN THE SIGNS: Approximately every two and a half days, the Moon moves from one zodiac sign to the next. The sign that the Moon is in at the beginning of the day (midnight Eastern Standard Time) is noted next to the quarter listing. If the Moon changes signs that day, there will be a notation saying "☽ enters" followed by the symbol for the sign it is entering.

MOON VOID-OF-COURSE: Just before the Moon enters a new sign, it will make one final aspect (angular relationship) to another planet. Between that last aspect and the entrance of the Moon into the next sign it is said to be void-of-course. Activities begun when the Moon is void-of-course rarely come to fruition, or they turn out very differently than planned.

Planetary Movement: When a planet or asteroid moves from one sign into another, this change (called an *ingress*) is noted on the calendar pages with the exact time. The Moon and Sun are considered planets in this case. The planets (except for the Sun and Moon) can also appear to move backward as seen from the Earth. This is called a *planetary retrograde*, and is noted on the calendar pages with the symbol ℞. When the planet begins to move forward, or direct, again, it is marked D, and the time is also noted.

Planting and Harvesting Days: The best days for planting and harvesting are noted on the calendar pages with a seedling icon (planting) and a basket icon (harvesting).

Time Zone Changes: The times and dates of all astrological phenomena in this datebook are based on Eastern time. If you live outside the Eastern time zone, you will need to make the following changes: Pacific Time subtract three hours; Mountain Time subtract two hours; Central Time subtract one hour; Alaska subtract four hours; and Hawaii subtract five hours. All data is adjusted for Daylight Saving Time.

Planets

☉	Sun	♆	Neptune
☽	Moon	♇	Pluto
☿	Mercury	⚷	Chiron
♀	Venus	⚳	Ceres
♂	Mars	⚴	Pallas
♃	Jupiter	⚵	Juno
♄	Saturn	⚶	Vesta
♅	Uranus		

1st Quarter/New Moon ☽
2nd Quarter ☽

Signs

♈	Aries	♐	Sagittarius
♉	Taurus	♑	Capricorn
♊	Gemini	♒	Aquarius
♋	Cancer	♓	Pisces
♌	Leo		
♍	Virgo		
♎	Libra		
♏	Scorpio		

Motion

℞ Retrograde
D Direct

3rd Quarter/Full Moon ☺
4th Quarter ☾

☽ **Tuesday** ← Day and date
1st ♎ ← Moon's quarter and sign
2nd Quarter 4:01 am ← Moon quarter change
☽ v/c 4:01 am ← Moon void-of-course
☽ enters ♏ 9:30 am ← Moon sign change/ingress
♄ ℞ 10:14 am ← Planetary retrograde
Color: Gray ← Color of the day

Planting day → 🌱

Harvesting day → 🧺

Magical Clothing
by Abby Willowroot

A Full Moon shines, the breeze picks up, and caped figures gather to celebrate in ritual and song. All are dressed in fine ritual wear bought at Renaissance fairs or from magical vendors, but few are wearing truly magical garments of power. Truly powerful magical garments must contain the physical essence, perceptions, and intention of the wearer's spirit.

This psychic investment can only be achieved through the actions of the wearer. You cannot buy it or trade for it. While these wonderful cloaks and other clothing offered for sale are a great place to start, what you add to them—and the way you do it—is what will transform a beautiful, but impersonal, garment into a powerful and extraordinary one. Ancient shamans, priestesses, wizards, and healers adorned themselves and their clothing with things that held special meaning for them, things that held power and expressed the spirit of magic.

Your spirit and your journey are like no one else's; you are a unique expression of the universe's energy. Why should your magical adornments and clothing be manufactured just like thousands of others? Any cloak can easily be adorned with beads, shells, thread, ribbon, or other personal effects to make it the expression of your own magical journey. The more you focus your energy into a piece of clothing, the more powerfully charged it will become for your magical work.

The first rule of living a magical life is claiming your own power and learning to trust your own perceptions. All magic and spell work flow from this simple beginning. Just as creating an altar is a way of defining your ritual workspace, adding ornaments to your clothing can define your sacred personal body space.

Creating magical garments is like a blessing spell you cast over yourself and your ritual work. Each stitch, each bead, each detail has a transformative power that adds deeper meaning and potency to your garment. Like planting a garden, the work put into a piece of magical clothing can grow to become beautiful and soul nurturing. All who see such a handworked piece will be enriched and enchanted by its uniqueness and beauty.

Visualize your personal magical clothing in meditation or ritual. Ask the universe to guide you in creating it. Be open to influences from different cultures and eras—even different aspects of yourself. Opening yourself to this creativity is the beginning of a mystical journey of exploration that will last a lifetime. What you create now will likely evolve over time as you wear it in rituals and celebrations.

There is no end to the wonderful pieces of ritual clothing you can create. If you sew, that is great, but sewing is not essential—manufactured clothing is OK. The base clothing you use for your magical ritual wear can be anything you like, as long as the fabric is strong enough to carry the adornments you add to it without ripping or sagging.

An ordinary cloak can be painted, beaded, embroidered, appliquéd, or ornamented along the hem, around the hood, across the back, or left plain on the outside and elaborately decorated on the inside. You can create anything you can imagine. Often, the final design can stem from the first embellishment, so sit with the item you want to make more powerful, and in time your inspiration will come.

Starting Your Magical Wardrobe

A beautiful shoulder mantle can be made with a simple piece of square fabric one yard long. Versatile garments, shoulder mantles can be worn over any dress, shirt, or robe, making them a good place to start if you aren't sure what you want to do. Choose sturdy velvet, cotton, or other comfortable fabric with a tight weave that will drape well. Fold the fabric in half (straight or diagonally), cut a slit in the center of the folded edge for a head hole, and finish the edge with stitches or iron-on binding tape. The outside edges can be finished in the same way, or frayed to make a short fringe. Before you begin adding to the mantle, ask yourself a few simple questions.

What is important to me? Do I like simple or fancy? Do I want subtle or bright colors? Do I want things hanging down from the mantle or not? Do I want a woodsy feel or a more urban feel? Ancient or futuristic? Do I want to add items to my mantle over time? Do I want to make it for all rituals or do I want a specific element like earth, air, fire, or water? Do I want to dedicate it to a specific goddess or god? Do I want to make an animal energy shamanic mantle? Do I want my mantle to jingle or make a sound when I walk? Do I want to use paints or not? Once you know the answers to these questions, you will know how to create a mantle that is uniquely yours.

For a natural ocean feel, you can add shells—loose shells from inexpensive shell necklaces are great because the shells are already drilled. If you live near the ocean, try adding dried seaweed, tiny drift-wood pieces, or beach glass. Seashores and riverbanks can offer some amazing treasures that are perfect for your purposes. You can also add blue, aqua, green, or sandy-colored beads, thread, or ribbons, which can be sewn or tied on with embroidery floss (thread) or clear fish line. You will need to poke a hole in the fabric with a thick needle to put the floss or line through when tying pieces to the fabric. If you hot-glue items to your clothing, it is a good idea to also add a bit of thread over three sides of the piece to make sure they stay in place.

A wooded-grove feel can be created using small fallen twigs, dried moss, seedpods, acorns or other nuts, as well as long strands of grass or wheat, which can be woven or braided. Fresh leaves or flower petals can be ironed between two sheets of wax paper to preserve them, then cut out and sprayed with lacquer to seal them and to prevent melted wax from seeping out later. Small stones can be wrapped with floss and hung so they sway slightly and clink together softly when you move. Bark, willow roots, beads—you can use just about anything you like.

Feathers can also be used in interesting ways, but feathers should always be decontaminated by washing and letting them dry, and then spraying with a tick and chigger repellent spray. This is very important because bird feathers have many types of parasites. (If you want to skip this step, store-bought feathers have already been cleaned and treated.) Once cleaned, feathers can be added individually or in rows to create an amazing garment. Beads can be slipped onto the quill before sewing or tying into place.

For a more futuristic feel, silver-colored washers with a center hole can be tied onto the mantle, and beads can be placed in the hole. Chips, circuits, and other computer parts, metal bits, holographic fabric, brass items, parts from broken appliances, and tiny mirrors can be added. Wire can be braided or woven together in all kinds of shapes.

Finally, and perhaps most importantly, personal treasures often make wonderful additions to ritual clothing. Charms, crystal pendants, amulets, small sturdy keepsakes, buttons, or bits of fabric from cherished clothes or old ritual garments can be added. Mementos of childhood or special moments also can find a place in your ritual wardrobe. Painting your ritual clothes with acrylic or fabric paints is also a wonderful way to make them your own. Painted scenes, creatures, goddesses, Green Man, magical symbols, or simple areas of color and texture work well. You are the creator and whatever you are drawn to create will be an expression of your magical self.

These suggestions will work equally well for cloaks, robes, pants, tunics, shoes, or any other kind of magical clothing. Cloaks with Celtic interlaces can be ornamented by edging the interlaces in gold and silver thread.

One of the most wonderful ways to create a powerful piece of ritual clothing is to add a momento from each ritual you participate in—a pebble, a twig, stone, flower petal, ribbon, or bit of fabric. Every time you put your magical garment on, you will be calling forth the energy and power of all those past rituals and celebrations and wrapping yourself in their power. Whatever you create, may you walk in magic always!

The Sacred Flame
by Diana Rajchel

Whether a Celtic goddess, the foster mother of Christ, or an accidental bishop of the Irish Catholic church, Brigid carried with her an association that crossed generations: flame. Hundreds of years past the point where anyone could definitively verify her existence, a convent of women tend her flame, and pilgrims light candles from this fire in hopes of carrying a little power to their homelands. Fire, unchangeable but changing everything, has made Brigid immortal. Even if she were fiction, the eternal flame has made her a truth.

Of all the elements, fire stands the furthest from humanity. We can see it and feel it, but we can't hold it—and we can't survive without it. Our very lives are powered by flame. The Sun, a giant floating ball of flame, generates light and heat so plants can process their food and subsequently become food for other creatures. Fire is primal. It is life. It is food.

Ancient mythologies are filled with stories of humans obtaining fire. In the tale of Prometheus, a Greek titan took great personal risk and from the Sun stole fire, which he gave to humanity in defiance of a dictate from the ruling gods. Because of his gift, the ancient Greeks attributed the whole of their civilization to Prometheus. With fire, they could cook, seek shelter against the cold, and have an advantage over animals. The symbolism of fire as power, knowledge, and independence is woven throughout the tale—leaving the impression that human beings could not have evolved without fire.

10

Yet, like all powerful tools, fire comes with a price. Fire can only exist by burning some other element, usually some composite of earth and air, such as wood. Its transformative effects have a byproduct, from the smell after cauterizing a wound to particles released into the air upon burning wood. With fire comes sterilization, yet fire is the catalyst that produces most air pollution. To the ancient Greeks, fire brought the first

vestiges of a civilized society. But it also made possible the production of tools through melting metals in extreme heat, and with tools came the production of weapons, and with weapons, the advent of war.

Nearly all aspects of living have at least a duality, some sort of light and shadow, and fire's light and shadow is, by its nature, the one that contrasts most starkly. In witchcraft, nearly all tools, elements, and divinities have a dark side. As Z. Budapest once said, "a Witch who can't hex, can't heal," or to paraphrase, an athame that can't cut isn't good for good and certainly isn't good for bad. Since the candle flame is arguably the most used tool in the practice of witchcraft, it's only fitting that it in particular holds both danger and benefit.

Witches can draw on the power of flame, their own little patch of Sun, for almost any religious or magical reason. Witches on e-mail groups practice candle keeping, in which each person takes a turn maintaining a flame to raise prayers and benefits to the gods, to the elementals, or to nature itself. It's a logical action from a magical/sky worship perspective. Heat rises, so what better way to raise prayers than to burn a candle that releases a flame ever upward? Fire and flame also encourage speed. There's no such thing as burning in slow motion. So when something must be accomplished *right now*, burning a candle or lighting a fire ignites that action because flame can never be still.

Because flame comes directly from the Sun that generates all life, it follows that fire itself lives. As the only element that manifests close to its pure form, fire gives the appearance of being independently sentient. Ceremonial magicians may look for salamanders, small creatures that live within the flame, that they might command and direct. Muslim ceremonial magicians may look for evidence of djinn, beings that are parallel to humans but composed completely of fire. Fire is always life, and like life, can be dangerous—because of that, fire is also death.

As a volatile double-edged sword, the impact of fire plays prominently in many religions. Judeo-Christians have the sanctity and potency of fire spelled out repeatedly in their scriptures, with frequent instances of theophany appearing throughout the Old and New Testaments. In Genesis, God's division of light and darkness to divide night and day is interpreted as a manifestation of flame; angels guarding the Garden of Eden are said to have held flaming swords (symbolizing empowerment of God), and God manifested to Moses in his mystic vision as a burning bush. The baptism of Christ, when clouds parted and marked Jesus with sunlight upon the completion of the act, is also viewed as the force of God making itself known through fire. Orthodox Christians interpret these stories as God "shining a light unto the path," and even celebrate a Feast of the Theophany, a day parishioners bring small containers to church for the holy water (empowered by the prayer to/fire of God). Later on, a parish priest comes by and performs a blessing on their homes. While Protestants rarely engage in this level of ritual and folkway, many denominations do keep a candle burning on or near the altar, that either the clergy or the congregation continuously feeds with oil so that it never burns out. Called the eternal flame, it is regarded as a continuous connection to God.

Jewish tradition venerates flame as one of God's great miracles, particularly during Hanukkah, "the Festival of Lights." After a ruler of Israel attempted to outlaw Judaism and tried to convert a temple to the worship of Zeus, a small band of Jewish men rebelled and eventually overthrew the ruler. One of the men who revolted became the new ruler of Israel, and in his duty as a priest-king, he set about reco-

vering the violated temple. At this time, oil was low for a menorah, but it had to burn day and night as a fire-vigil to God. Miraculously, the menorah continued to burn for eight days, until enough oil to refresh the flame arrived. Modern-day worshipers celebrate Hanukkah by lighting a single light each day over the course of eight days. The only purpose for these candles or oil lamps is to meditate upon

Hanukkah; if a dedicatee wishes to do anything else, an extra light must be placed near the menorah.

Wiccans celebrate a series of fire festivals distributed throughout the sabbat cycle; they are frequently called "crossquarters" as holidays that fall on neither solstice nor equinox. Imbolc, Beltane, Lammas, and Samhain all mark significant points in the Wiccan cyclical mythos, and the symbolism and effect of flame changes within that mythos. Imbolc marks a beginning. Celebrated right at the edge of winter's tightest grip, the sabbat honors the inching return of the Sun as a sign that spring will come and give relief from the aching cold and that survival, for a little while, will be easier. Wiccans often celebrate the day by engaging in crafts such as candle- and incense-making, or by planning what they'll do with their gardens as soon as the first frost breaks. By the time the wheel turns to Beltane, the Sun is in the sky, spring is in the air, and survival is of a more carnal nature. At Beltane, fires are kindled outdoors as a representation of the Sun kindling life and encouraging procreation. Wiccans may celebrate their commitment to their lovers by jumping over the fire with a partner or partners, and also make use of the heat generated within their own bodies for more private celebrations. At Lammas, the Sun has subtly begun inching its way down in the sky, and even at the hottest part of summer, thoughts turn to planning for winter survival in harsher conditions. The fires (or, more often, barbecues) are recognized as a way of reaping the harvest by transforming the growth and hunt into food, and it's silently understood that it will get colder soon. Samhain marks the end of summer, and the fire is viewed as a sort of funeral pyre—the catalyst that transforms the body into the ash, making it the most easily consumed back into the earth. It is the death of the year—the final transformation that must happen for the year to continue and for human beings to survive.

Fire is the most primal and purest manifestation of energy we experience on this plane. It brings both death and life; it can harm and heal; and we rely on it for protection and as a weapon. Fire, as the untouchable but clearly present force, connects to the divine in a more visual and visceral manner than any other element. Its power, its necessity, and its danger are undeniable.

An Astrological Look at 2008

by K. D. Spitzer

To see the winds of change for the coming year, an astrologer will cast a chart for the moment when the Sun enters Capricorn, usually on December 21. For many of us, that date marks the festival of Yule and it is a wise Pagan who plans to incorporate some of this astrological energy into ritual. It is usual to cast the chart for Washington, D.C., the seat of the federal government.

This year the Sun is going to change signs a little late. It is almost exactly partnering Jupiter and Mercury, with Pluto, still in Sagittarius and breathing down their necks (think Darth Vader), right behind them. So it's in the early hours of December 22 (1:05 am EST to be exact) that the Sun finally leaves Sagittarius and eases into Capricorn.

After the tumultuous year 2007, we are going to be working hard on our relationships. Libra is on the Ascendant, therefore Venus is ruling most activities during 2008. Venus wants everyone to look good and to get along, but since she's in Scorpio, she may be feeling a little passive-aggressive. She's not the most comfortable in this sign, but is very happy to be sitting in her own Second House of money and values. Also she's getting soothing help from Uranus (if there is such a thing) and both are lending all the qualities of the element of water to the Midheaven. With little bumps in the road here and there—because Uranus "needs" excitement—things look pretty good, you would think.

Retrograde Mars is sitting in the house of foreign travel and all dressed up in Cancerian watercolors. You would think that we're looking at a peaceful and diplomatic year ahead. However, Mars is being fueled by that little package of planets that moved into Capricorn across the zodiac. If nothing else, his relationship to Mercury will cause conversation to be very interesting—sometimes shrill, sometimes harsh, and most often misinterpreted. He will also want to be on the offensive.

The Sun in Capricorn is standing foursquare next to Jupiter, who wants to expand all the qualities (good and bad) of that authoritarian Sun. With Mars standing with his fists on his hips and glaring across at them, you can sure bet that our national identity is going to be challenged, and maybe even hotly contested. And with the Moon in mutable Gemini and approaching the halfway mark in its cycle, responses may be quick and not well thought out.

On the other hand, the Moon's Nodes are sitting quietly in the karmic degree of Aquarius (29 degrees). Since the Nodes are karmic indicators in a chart, this tells us we're looking at an especially important year. Saturn, that other karmic planet, is sitting on a very sensitive point and retrograding through Virgo in a wide inconjunction with the Nodes. We definitely need to make right some previous wrongs and, if possible, set some positive karma into motion. The universe is demanding it. Fortunately, Saturn will bring a huge dose of reality to all our posturing and, we can only hope, may even bring common sense to our actions on the world stage.

By the Spring Equinox, Mars is still in Cancer and now direct, but he has moved around to the Seventh House of relationships and open enemies. This time he is trying to stare down Darth Vader (you know, Pluto in a black cloak and storm trooper boots) and both of them are trying to egg on the Sun to aggressively take risks. All three of them need to develop a healthy and safe outlet for all this dark energy. It is possible to take assertive action without aggression.

The Moon is still a few degrees from being full and it's in critically discerning Virgo, which should be a big help, but she can't decide if she wants us to take care of our own needs or look out for the needs of others. With other planets giving her the elbow to get her attention, she needs to focus on keeping a balance in her emotions—and so do we. Suddenly getting upset is possible, which is not a good thing, so we need to take care not to speak before thinking.

Eclipses are always important in the chart of a country and its people, although some years more than others. Mostly we have two solar eclipses and two lunar eclipses in a year. The lunar eclipses are about two weeks before or after the solar ones. The solar ones require a New Moon and the lunar eclipses always involve the Full Moon.

Prior to Yule, the September 11, 2007, solar eclipse is going to have an impact on the country lasting several years. It is the anniversary date of 9/11, but it also falls on a critical point in Virgo that was first activated in the Sixties. (Astrology is all about planetary cycles—what they did in the past and how they will behave now.)

This eclipse will call for a return to some of the ideals of that time and as the outer planets wheel and turn in the sky, we edge toward health care for all, sustainable agriculture and other environmental concerns, along with many social and religious issues that have held stagnant in the status quo. As 2008 begins, Pluto has just moved to Capricorn and thus begins an important eclipse year. The planets in the eclipses sit on assorted planets in the U.S. chart.

As I mentioned earlier, the whole chart unrolls based upon the time of birth. Various astrologers have differing opinions on the time of day the Declaration of Independence was signed and all are prepared to heatedly defend it. Unfortunately, none of the guys in that sweltering room in Philadelphia wrote down the exact time; although later in journals or letters, some of them provided circumstantial (and conflicting) evidence. This has left the field wide open for everyone to choose the Ascendant that they feel reflects the national character.

Most astrologers like the Sagittarius rising chart showing the document was signed at 2:10 pm, although most the other times cited do work. The February solar eclipse in Aquarius falls right on the Moon of the country. The Moon represents us, the people, and places a strong emphasis on communication. The month before this eclipse, look for a very critical period in the presidential primary season; this will continue to dictate a wild and stormy ride to Election Day, which is subject to a Mercury station. Eeek!

Environmental issues will be paramount in the November election as concerns about food, fuel, weather, and air can no longer be ignored. We may even see major reform as people begin to demand it.

There is another solar eclipse in August and in this one, the Sun and Moon are sitting right on the North Node or Dragon's Head of the U.S. chart. This is karma driven and in the chart of a country, often foretells of aggressive action. At the very least, the finances of the country are going to be challenged.

A ritual for Yule 2007 should center on bringing back the light to the world soul. Light all your candles, deck your altar and greens with strings of lights, find that place within yourself that is content and serene, and project it outward for world peace. Join hands with others to help bring it about. Visualize a world without weapons. Think balance and harmony.

The New Moon/solar eclipse in Aquarius on February 6 portends changeable weather, with drought or flooding affecting food supplies worldwide. Ritual should sound the call for humanitarian efforts. As this decade moves to its conclusion, as ever, the main component of every ritual should be peace in the hearts of all humankind. Waning Moon rituals should be centered on letting go of fear and hatred.

The Lunar eclipse on February 20 will bring new military advances. The trend to eat locally is beginning to gather momentum. Plan a veggie garden to dedicate in Full Moon ritual. Self-reliance is a theme that will continue to gather mainstream speed; for many Pagans, it is already their lifestyle.

The eclipse in Leo on August 1 will need all the positive thinking we can provide to release fears. Hidden events, fraud, and naval mishaps will be coming to our attention. The Full Moon eclipse on

August 16 uncovers strange happenings and highlights the need for lasting social reform.

Lammas should not only celebrate the harvest, but exhort the grains to greater growth. As the country moves in the direction of ethanol as fuel, we need good weather and soil to supply our burgeoning need for corn.

Walk a labyrinth for each of your rituals to dedicate your spiritual work for a world spiraling toward peace. Find the goddess in the center and let her know you will join your energy to hers and others to restore harmony to our earth.

Charts

USA – Sibley: Koch July 4, 1776, 2:10 pm LMT, Philadelphia, PA.

Capricorn Ingress: Koch December 22, 2007, 1:06 am EST, Washington, D.C.

Solar Eclipse/Virgo: Koch September 11, 2007, 8:44 am EDT, Washington, D.C.

Solar Eclipse/Aquarius: Koch February 6, 2008, 10:44 pm EST, Washington, D.C.

Lunar Eclipse/Virgo: Koch February 20, 2008, 10:30 pm EST, Washington, D.C.

Solar Eclipse/Leo: Koch August 1, 2008, 6:12 am EDT, Washington, D.C.

Lunar Eclipse/Aquarius: Koch August 16, 2008, 5:16 pm EDT, Washington, D.C.

Lughnasadh: Koch August 6, 2008, 11:15 pm EDT, Washington, D.C.

Faery Magic: Best Times, Places

by Ellen Dugan

Hand in hand, with faery grace,
Will we sing, and bless this place.
—William Shakespeare, A Midsummer's Night Dream

It takes a certain kind of magic to believe in the realm of the faery. There has to be a deep and loving connection to the earth and an innocence of spirit. To discover the world of the Fey, you must let go of what you think you know and allow yourself to experience a whole other level of awareness. You must pay attention to all your senses, both physical and psychic, if you want to encounter the faeries. However, you can stack the odds in your favor once you realize that there are certain times, places, and days of the year when the veil between our world and the faery realm is thin. Faery activity is at its peak and it's here you are most likely to have the best luck viewing, contacting, and working with the faeries.

As to the proper time to communicate with or to work your faery spells and enchantments, go for the classic "in between" times. These 'tween times are at dawn, dusk, noon, and midnight. Dawn and dusk (or sunrise and sunset if you prefer) are the perfect 'tween times, as these moments in the day are neither one nor the other. It's somewhere magically between daylight and dark. Noon marks the smack-dab middle of the day. While many would never even consider trying a spell at noon, they need to open their eyes and to realize that magical opportunities surround them more frequently than they think. Sure, casting a spell at midnight is more likely to feel mysterious and witchy, but noon is a 'tween time too. Is it morning or night, or is it both? On the flip side, midnight is the best known magical time. As it is neither night nor morning, one calendar day or the next, it actually hovers for a brief moment just in between the two. You could also consider New Year's Eve to be a special 'tween time as well!

So are we finished with our 'tween theme yet? Nope. We still have to take a look at the 'tween places in nature and around your home that are most likely to be hotbeds of faery activity. These are typically referred to as "faery haunts," the places most favored by the faeries.

The general rule of thumb when it comes to faery haunts is to look for the outdoor places that are also in between, such as a stream or riverbank. If you are standing on the banks, then you are neither in the water or on dry land, you are in between, same thing goes for ocean beaches and lake shorelines. Faeries are found in more places than just the forest; they like the water as well. Also keep your eyes open if you happen to be in a place where streams intersect or divide, and geographical areas where two or three rivers meet. These are natural, powerful, and sacred spaces.

The garden and the local woods, as you'd imagine, also provide you with many excellent opportunities for working with the faeries. Nature spirits love the flowers, so whether they grow in your backyard garden, you stumble across a little cluster of wildflowers tucked under a tree in the woods, or you happen across a field of wildflowers, faery activity will be present. Also, consider the hedgerows, under a tree in the park, and at a crossroads in your neighborhood, or even under

the stairs in your house. Oh, and we shouldn't forget that thresholds and doorways are prime faery spots as well.

It is certainly true that the faeries are out and about all the time and on every day of the year. However, there are days and then there are "days." Now as you would imagine, the eight sabbats are prime faery days. So are the nights of the Full Moon, including the occasional Blue

Moon. Also, some texts claim that you will find success if you work on the day of the New Moon as well.

The following dates of the solstices and equinoxes are correct for 2008. Remember, for future reference, that the solstice and equinox dates will change from year to year, depending on when the beginning of specific astrological signs occur. Following these dates are the type of faeries and nature spirit energies you are likely to encounter at that point of the wheel of the year.

New Year's Day, January 1

The faeries of winter are out and about at this time of year. These nature spirits show you the beauty found when chilly rains, snow, and ice covers the land. Jack Frost is a well-known faery spirit and this is his busiest time of the year. Watch for the pictures he will paint on your windows in the mornings and see what you can discover.

Imbolc, February 2

The Snow Queen is holding court at this time of the year. Even as we reach the halfway point between winter and spring and celebrate the strengthening light, her Highness is reigning supreme and "blessing" us with the heaviest of snows and coldest temperatures of the year. Use this time for introspection, making plans, and personal development.

Ostara (Vernal Equinox), March 20

The faeries of spring have arrived and they are some of the fiercest energies you will encounter in nature. Spring is often portrayed as a gentle season; however, it takes a great deal of power and strength to break out of winter's hold and burst forth in new growth and color. Work with the nature spirits now to bring about transformation and to help new projects grow and flourish.

Lady Day, March 25

Rejoice in the blooming crocus, daffodils, and the earliest of flowers. This is the Lady's day and her nature spirits are busy everywhere in nature, encouraging the plants to grow and the humans to tap into this magical energy and to use it wisely for a little personal growth of their own.

Beltane Eve, April 30

According to faery lore, Beltane Eve marks the date of a leprechaun festival. This is a classic 'tween time second only to the night of Samhain. Call on the leprechauns for prosperity and good luck. Leave a few tumbled stones for them in thanks for their assistance.

Beltane, May 1

One of the biggest days of the year for faery activity. The faeries are out in force so make sure you are respectful of their powers. This is the time to enjoy their presence—not to make requests. Work with garden flowers to appease the Fey. If you worry about being "faery led" or tricked, wear a chaplet of violets, or tuck a sprig of St. John's wort in your hair.

Midsummer / Summer Solstice, June 20

A prime time for working magic with the Fey. This day is not only sacred to the faery, but to lovers everywhere. At the close of the longest day, settle someplace in the wild for an attempt at viewing the faeries at dusk on a romantic Midsummer's evening.

Lammas, August 1

Celebrate the beginning of the harvest season by leaving out an offering to the faeries in your yard. A small plate of plain cookies will work nicely. If you ask politely, they will offer you and your family protection during the hottest days of the year, and possibly grant protection from wild summer thunderstorms.

Mabon / Autumn Equinox, September 22

As the season of autumn rolls in, keep a watchful eye on nature as she begins her big show of the year with all the blazing autumn colors. The faeries of the fall are busy now, adding color to the landscape, coaxing the last of the flowers to bloom, and painting dewdrops on the morning grass. Leave out a small saucer of milk on a fine autumn evening in gratitude for all the nature spirit's hard work as the harvest is gathered.

Samhain / Halloween, October 31

At Samhain the doorways are flung open between our world, the spirit plane, and the faery realm. While the Fey are easiest to contact on this night, I suggest both respect and caution. It is suggested that you carry thistle with you for protection, as anything is possible tonight. Light candles inside of your jack-o'-lanterns now for their original

purpose—to frighten off bad luck and trickery from the more mischievous faeries.

Yule / Winter Solstice, December 21

The shortest day and longest night of the year invite ample opportunities for the faeries to become a vital part of this season. The Fey have been hard at work coaxing nature to sleep as winter begins. So keep in mind that there are faeries and nature spirits who enjoy coming inside now and hanging out in the Yule trees and fresh pine greenery and holly that decorate many a home at this festive time of year. Welcome them in and accept that your holidays will become more magical.

Create and Use Thoughtforms
by Gerina Dunwich

A thoughtform (a.k.a. a servitor or an egregore) is an artificial elemental that is intentionally created through visualization and infused with emotional energy. They are nonmaterial creatures and consist of astral substance, or ether. Though frequently an overlooked aspect of contemporary magical training, many Witches and other practitioners of the magical arts have employed thoughtforms since ancient times. Thoughtforms have been described as "vortexes" or "centers of psychic energy," and can take on the appearance of an animal, a human, or any type of mythical creature their creators visualize.

Although relatively simple to create, they can aid a magical practitioner in nearly all forms of spell work, including healings. They can serve as watchers, messengers, and even companions. (However, it should be made quite clear that a thoughtform is not the same thing as an imaginary friend.) Some people also create them to guard their homes, gardens, sacred spaces, and other areas.

Thoughtforms can also be unconsciously created, even by those who do not believe in the magical arts, when intense emotions (such as love or hatred) are directed at a specific individual for an extended time.

Found throughout history the world over, thoughtforms can be benign, demonic, or neutral. Ghosts, genies, angelic beings, Witches' familiars, and even the ancient gods and goddesses are types of thoughtforms. So too are the infamous seventy-two Goetic demons that were summoned and bound by the sorcerer King Solomon in olden times.

How to Create a Thoughtform

The following instructions are for creating a simple thoughtform and are designed with the beginner in mind. Advanced thoughtforms, on the other hand, should be left to individuals who possess the proper magical training and experience.

First, you must decide if you want your thoughtform to take the shape of a human, an animal, or some other creature. (An anthropomorphic or zoomorphic thoughtform is also known as a tulpa in the Tibetan tradition.) Keep in mind the purpose for which the thoughtform is being created and then choose the most appropriate form.

Next, find a quiet, comfortable place to visualize your thoughtform, and ritually purify it using salt, a smoldering sage bundle, or another method you are comfortable using. Light a candle of a color corresponding to the specific intent of your thoughtform. For instance: white for protection or healing; red for strength, passion, or confrontation; black for binding negative forces and uncrossing; purple for occult wisdom and psychic enhancement; silver for astral and dream work; and so forth.

Using whatever technique works best for you, allow your mind to enter an alpha state. Begin rhythmic breathing and clear your mind of all mundane thoughts. When you feel totally relaxed and are unable to feel your physical body, you are ready to begin visualization.

With your eyes closed, visualize a glowing ball of light floating in the air in front of you, then use your will to make it take on the color associated with your intent. Once this is complete, use your will to transform the sphere into the specific shape you desire, taking care not to overlook small details such as hair and eye color, garments, etc. It is also a good idea to equip your thoughtform with the appropriate tool or tools required for its intended job. For instance, a thoughtform that is programmed for healing purposes could be equipped with a special charm bag containing powerful medicinal herbs or healing gemstones.

As you visualize, chant your intent and infuse the thoughtform with as much emotional energy as you can raise. This is best done by channeling energy through your solar plexus chakra (midway between the navel and the base of the sternum).

Some magical practitioners also find that the act of visualizing symbols, such as runes or bind-runes, upon their thoughtforms empowers them with extra energy, thus allowing them to carry out their missions faster and with much better results.

The next step is to give your thoughtform a name. This is an important part of its creation process, for naming your artificial elemental will allow you to exercise more control over it. The name you choose should be unusual and unique to prevent other people from using it and summoning your thoughtform. Repeat the name several times, either out loud or telepathically.

The thoughtform is now ready to be charged and sent forth to do its work, or stored for future use. For the latter, some practitioners prefer to house their thoughtforms in crystals or talismans. However, a small empty bottle or box will work just fine, especially if it is inscribed with the elemental symbol corresponding to the thoughtform. To store the thoughtform, hold in your hand the object in which you wish to keep it and then use your will to direct the thoughtform into it. After it has been stored in its container, put it in a safe place where it will not be disturbed. Hold it often and charge it with energy to prevent the thoughtform within it from dissipating.

Summoning the thoughtform can be done by simply uttering or thinking its name. Do not be concerned if you are unable to see the thoughtform appear before you. Most are not visible to the naked eye and can be perceived only by those who possess the power of clairvoyant vision. Although you may not be able to directly observe it, you will probably be able to feel its presence.

How to Charge and Send Forth a Thoughtform

Now that your thoughtform has been created, it is ready to be charged and sent forth to carry out its intended work. The best time to do this is when the Moon is in a waxing phase or full, as these lunar influences can bolster the energy of your charging ritual.

Charging a thoughtform requires concentrating on your intent and using the power of emotional energy to direct the focused outcome into the artificial elemental. Using a short sentence consisting of no more than five words, telepathically instruct the thoughtform what to do. (It is best to keep your commands simple because intentionally created thoughtforms do not respond well to complex and detailed instructions.) After commanding the thoughtform, release it into the void like a bullet shot from a gun.

The success (or failure) of a thoughtform depends mainly upon the mind strength and aura of the person who creates it. Like any other type of magical working, the more energy and faith you put into it, the greater results you will achieve. But if your energy level and faith in your abilities as a magical worker are low, a weak thoughtform that will dissipate very quickly and accomplish very little, if anything at all, is probably the best that you can hope for.

In many cases, after a thoughtform has completed its mission or runs out of energy, it will dissolve on its own into the ethers. To keep it from dissipating, you need to perform regular recharging sessions. In some cases, a symbiotic link between the thoughtform and either its creator or target can also keep it charged. Thoughtforms can also feed off of energy sources other than their creators, mutate from the accumulation of various outside influences, and return to wreak havoc. This is why it is always a good idea to undo your thoughtforms once you are finished working with them or if you create one in error.

How to Undo a Thoughtform

When you no longer need your thoughtform, you should undo it and return the energy to Mother Earth to prevent its stray energy from rebounding and bringing about undesired effects. To do this, allow your mind to enter an alpha state on a night when the Moon is in a waning phase. (This is the appropriate lunar phase during which to perform spells and rituals for the elimination of unwanted things.) Summon the thoughtform by calling its name and visualize it floating in the air above you. Then visualize it deconstructing in the reverse order in which it was constructed and then dissipating like mist into the air. As you do this, recite the following incantation, or whatever words you feel are appropriate: "Elemental, you have served me well. The time has come to end this spell. Energy unweave; intent disperse. I cast you back into the earth. As I will it, so mote it be."

Keep in mind that the more powerful a thoughtform becomes, the more effort it will require on the part of its creator to undo it. You may have to repeat the ritual several times before the thoughtform is completely eliminated.

December/January

◐ Monday

3rd ♎︎
4th quarter 2:51 am
♂ enters ♊︎ 11:00 am
Color: White

New Year's Eve
Castle of Countess Barthory of Hungary
raided, 1610; accused of practicing black
magic, she murdered scores of the local
townsfolk; she was walled up in a room in
her castle, where she later died

1 Tuesday

4th ♎︎
☽ v/c 7:33 pm
☽ enters ♏︎ 8:32 pm
Color: Maroon

New Year's Day
Kwanzaa ends
Birthday of Sir James Frazer,
author of *The Golden Bough*, 1854

2 Wednesday

4th ♏︎
Color: White

3 Thursday

4th ♏︎
☽ v/c 7:30 pm
Color: Purple

Death of Edgar Cayce, psychic, 1945

4 Friday

4th ♏︎
☽ enters ♐︎ 9:13 am
Color: Coral

Aquarian Tabernacle Church
registered in Australia by
Lady Tamara Von Forslun, 1994

28   *Set in Eastern Standard Time (EST)*

5 Saturday

4th ♐
Color: Indigo

6 Sunday

4th ♐
☽ v/c 7:27 pm
☽ enters ♑ 8:43 pm
Color: Orange

Twelfth Night/Epiphany

Patricia Crowther's witchcraft
radio show, *A Spell of Witchcraft*,
airs in Britain, 1971

January

7 Monday
4th ♑
☿ enters ♒ 11:46 pm
Color: Gray

☽ Tuesday
4th ♑
☽ v/c 6:37 am
New Moon 6:37 am
Color: White

Birthday of MacGregor Mathers,
one of the three original founders
of the Golden Dawn, 1854
Death of Dion Fortune, 1946

9 Wednesday
1st ♑
☽ enters ♒ 6:13 am
Color: Yellow

Jamie Dodge wins lawsuit against
the Salvation Army, which fired her
based on her Wiccan religion, 1989

10 Thursday
1st ♒
Color: Green

Islamic New Year

11 Friday
1st ♒
☽ v/c 12:52 pm
☽ enters ♓ 1:44 pm
Color: Pink

Set in Eastern Standard Time (EST)

The Craft of the Wise

Witchcraft weaves the world we know,
East and South and West and North.
Summer's bloom and winter's snow,
With our rites we call them forth.

Tools of magic we command
Yet the power lies within
Mind and spirit, head and hand,
Not the objects, thick or thin.

God and Goddess, two yet One,
In Their unity made whole,
Through the circles we have spun,
Teach us secrets of the soul.
　　　　　　　—Elizabeth Barrette

12 Saturday

1st ♓
Color: Blue

Mary Smith hanged in England;
she had quarreled with neighbors,
who said that the Devil appeared
to her as a black man, 1616

13 Sunday

1st ♓
☽ v/c 6:41 pm
☽ enters ♈ 7:23 pm
Color: Yellow

Final witchcraft laws
repealed in Austria, 1787

January

14 Monday
1st ♈
Color: Lavender

Official Confession of Error by
jurors of Salem Witch Trials, 1696

Human Be-In, a Pagan-style festival,
takes place in San Francisco, attended by
Timothy Leary and Allen Ginsburg, 1967

◑ Tuesday
1st ♈
2nd quarter 2:46 pm
☽ v/c 10:39 pm
☽ enters ♉ 11:13 pm
Color: Black

16 Wednesday
2nd ♉
Color: Topaz

Birthday of Dr. Dennis Carpenter,
Circle Sanctuary

17 Thursday
2nd ♉
☽ v/c 9:05 pm
Color: Turquoise

*A happy life is one which is
in accordance with its own nature*

18 Friday
2nd ♉
☽ enters ♊ 1:30 am
Color: Rose

Set in Eastern Standard Time (EST)

Imbolc Cleansing Curry

2 T. olive oil
2 T. curry powder
1 tsp. whole mustard seeds
1 onion, chopped
1 can of coconut milk
1 cup of water
2 medium potatoes, cubed
1 sweet potato, cubed
2 large carrots, sliced
2 cups green beans, sliced
1 cup of frozen peas
1 can of chickpeas, drained
1 tsp. salt
½ cup chopped cilantro (optional)

Heat oil in a large pot. Add curry powder and mustard seeds. When seeds pop, add the onion and sauté. Add coconut milk and water, then bring to a boil. Simmer until thickened. Add potatoes, sweet potatoes, beans, peas, carrots, and chickpeas. Simmer 20 to 30 minutes until vegetables are tender. Salt to taste. Garnish with cilantro if desired.

Put all your vegetables into this curry. Let the heat clear your head and the taste clear your palate. Get ready for the coming season of growth.

—Dallas Jennifer Cobb

19 Saturday
2nd ♊
Color: Brown

Birthday of Dorothy Clutterbuck,
who initiated Gerald Gardner, 1880

20 Sunday
2nd ♊
☽ v/c 2:46 am
☽ enters ♋ 3:05 am
☉ enters ♒ 11:43 am
Color: Gold

Sun enters Aquarius

January

21 Monday

2nd ♋
☽ v/c 5:56 am
Color: White

Birthday of Martin Luther King, Jr.
(observed)

Celtic Tree Month of Rowan begins

☺ Tuesday

2nd ♋
☽ enters ♌ 5:20 am
Full Moon 8:35 am
Color: Scarlet

Cold Moon

23 Wednesday

3rd ♌
Color: Brown

24 Thursday

3rd ♌
♀ enters ♑ 3:06 am
☽ v/c 9:43 am
☽ enters ♍ 9:48 am
Color: Purple

There are five steps to enlightenment:
listen, see, dream, love, and follow your heart

25 Friday

3rd ♍
♇ enters ♑ 9:37 pm
Color: Coral

Birthday of Robert Burns, Scottish poet, 1759

Leo Moon

The new year is a good time to leave old disagreements behind and to perform a ritual to end a long-standing argument or separation. The final aspect of this Full Moon is Moon trine Pluto. Trine final aspects are good for positive outcomes, and Pluto is associated with the unconscious, the hidden. With the Moon in Leo, a demonstrative or enthusiastic ritual is desired.

Since it is easier to perform the ritual first, then approach the person to heal the rift, a solitary ritual may be best. Choose an object(s) to represent those from whom you are divided. Items of sentimental value work well, but you may also use tarot cards based on the person and your relationship. Most decks explain what sort of person the Queen of Cups represents, but you should use the Hermit card if it fits the person better.

Go to your ritual space and cast a simple circle. Then face the object you have chosen to represent the estranged person. Talk to it, explain your feelings, and ask for reunion. Think about his or her point of view, try to put yourself in his or her place. End by saying, "For the good of all concerned." Cleanse the item used. Then contact that person to reconnect.

—Magenta Griffith

26 Saturday

3rd ♍
☽ v/c 6:32 am
☽ enters ♎ 5:35 pm
Color: Indigo

27 Sunday

3rd ♎
Color: Amber

Grow a bird's nest fern in your home
to protect all within, especially any children

28 Monday

3rd ♎
☿ ℞ 3:31 pm
☽ v/c 4:47 pm
Color: Silver

29 Tuesday

3rd ♎
☽ enters ♏ 4:35 am
Color: Gray

*At Setsubun, around February 3, it is
considered lucky to eat the same number of
soybeans as your current age, plus one*

◖ Wednesday

4th ♏
4th quarter 12:03 am
♂ D 5:33 pm
Color: Yellow

*Birthday of Zsuzsanna E. Budapest,
feminist Witch*

31 Thursday

4th ♏
☽ v/c 3:34 am
☽ enters ♐ 5:08 pm
Color: Crimson

*Dr. Fian, believed to be the head
of the North Berwick Witches, found
guilty and executed for witchcraft in
Scotland by personal order of King
James VI (James I of England), 1591*

1 Friday

4th ♐
Color: Purple

Imbolc

Ancient lore claims that the conditions on Imbolc can indicate the weather for the next six weeks, but in reverse. A dreary Imbolc means clear and mild weather will follow.

This festival is associated with rebirth and fertility. *Imbolc* is an old Irish word meaning "ewe's milk" or "in the belly." Also known as Brigid's Day, this is a time to honor the Celtic goddess of fire, the church's patron saint of smithcraft, poetry, and healing. Honor the sacred feminine within. Make a Brigid's Cross to hang over your door to welcome her. With two sticks of equal length, form a cross and securely tie with silver and white ribbon. On your altar, burn white and silver candles and then take a few sips of milk from your chalice. Take the chalice outside and pour the remaining milk on the earth:

> *For Brigid Goddess*
> *I bless with milk the sacred earth,*
> *For Brigid you are invited*
> *To nurture us with healing, fertility, and gift of birth.*

—Emely Flak

2 Saturday

4th ♐
☽ v/c 5:21 pm
Color: Black

Imbolc
Groundhog Day
Leo Martello becomes a third-degree
Welsh traditionalist, 1973

3 Sunday

4th ♐
☽ enters ♑ 4:52 am
Color: Gold

Yue-lao, the Chinese Old Man in the Moon,
holds the power to predestine marriages

February

4 Monday
4th ♑
☽ v/c 1:20 pm
Color: Lavender

Imbolc crossquarter day
(Sun reaches 15° Aquarius)

5 Tuesday
4th ♑
☽ enters ♒ 2:10 pm
Color: Red

Mardi Gras

Wednesday
4th ♒
New Moon 10:44 pm
Color: Topaz

Ash Wednesday
Solar eclipse 10:56 pm, 17° ♒ 44'

7 Thursday
1st ♒
☽ v/c 10:50 am
☽ enters ♓ 8:46 pm
Color: Turquoise

Chinese New Year (rat)
Death of Thomas Aquinas, scholar who
wrote that heresy was a product of
ignorance and therefore criminal, and
who refuted the *Canon Episcopi*, 1274

8 Friday
1st ♓
Color: Coral

Birthday of Susun Weed, owner of
Wise Woman Publishing
Birthday of Evangeline Adams,
American astrologer, 1868

9 Saturday

1st ♓
☽ v/c 4:05 pm
Color: Brown

10 Sunday

1st ♓
☽ enters ♈ 1:17 am
Color: Yellow

Zsuzsanna Budapest arrested and later
convicted for fortunetelling, 1975

February

11 Monday
1st ♈
☽ v/c 8:00 pm
Color: Ivory

*Mountains in dreams mean you are struggling
against some type of obstacle or challenge*

12 Tuesday
1st ♈
☽ enters ♉ 4:34 am
Color: White

Gerald Gardner, founder
of the Gardnerian tradition,
dies of heart failure, 1964

○ Wednesday
1st ♉
2nd quarter 10:33 pm
Color: Brown

14 Thursday
2nd ♉
☽ v/c 12:05 am
☽ enters ♊ 7:19 am
Color: Purple

Valentine's Day
Elsie Blum, a farmhand from
Oberstedten, Germany, sentenced
to death for witchcraft, 1652

15 Friday
2nd ♊
Color: Pink

Pope Leo X issues papal bull to ensure that
the secular courts carry out executions
of Witches convicted by the Inquisition,
1521; the bull was a response to the courts'
refusal to carry out the work of the Church

The Wand

Wand of magic, rod of might
Hold the glow of magic's light

Faithful service unto Will,
Render, letting nothing spill

Focus all that lies within
Bright and sharp as any pin

Like a laser of the mind
Point the power, loose and bind

Wand of slender, polished wood
Send your energy for good!
　　　　　　　—Elizabeth Barrette

16　Saturday

2nd ♊
☽ v/c 5:17 am
☽ enters ♋ 10:12 am
Color: Gray

To go further at work,
try burning brown and red candles together

17　Sunday

2nd ♋
♀ enters ♒ 11:22 am
☽ v/c 4:13 pm
⚷ enters ♓ 5:22 pm
Color: Orange

February

18 Monday

2nd ♋
☽ enters ♌ 1:51 pm
☿ D 9:57 pm
Color: Silver

Presidents' Day (observed)
Celtic Tree Month of Ash begins

19 Tuesday

2nd ♌
☉ enters ♓ 1:49 am
Color: Gray

Sun enters Pisces

☺ Wednesday

2nd ♌
☽ v/c 12:52 pm
☽ enters ♍ 7:06 pm
Full Moon 10:30 pm
Color: Yellow

Quickening Moon
Lunar eclipse 10:27 pm, 1° ♍ 53'
Society for Psychical Research,
devoted to paranormal research,
founded in London, 1882

21 Thursday

3rd ♍
Color: Green

Birthday of Patricia Telesco,
Wiccan author
Stewart Farrar initiated into
Alexandrian Wicca, 1970
Death of Theodore Parker Mills, 1996

22 Friday

3rd ♍
☽ v/c 9:14 pm
Color: White

Birthday of Sybil Leek, Wiccan author, 1922

Virgo Moon

This Moon is not good for most ritual work—the final aspect of Moon square Mars could bring conflict—but the energy of the eclipse during this Full Moon makes it good for a quiet meditative ritual to bring out your hidden depths. With Moon in Virgo helping put your mental and emotional house in order, a ritual for self-examination and self-expression is appropriate, as is work to break bad habits.

To break a bad habit, you will need quiet space to yourself. Write down exactly what that habit is, why you want to stop, and what you will be able to do once the habit is gone. Bring this into your ritual space. Cast a circle if you wish. Comfortably sit or lie down. To completely relax, tense each part of your body, then release the tension. Start with your feet and work your way up to your head. When finished, take three long, deep breaths, letting out all the air each time. Let your mind rest a while, then visualize yourself without the habit. See yourself slender, smoke-free, or however you wish. Hold the image as long as possible; when the image starts to waver, immediately say, "For the good of all, so mote it be." If there is a circle, open it.

—Magenta Griffith

23 Saturday

3rd ♍
☽ enters ♎ 2:44 am
Color: Blue

The scents of lilac or gardenia can bring
more balance and harmony into your life

24 Sunday

3rd ♎
Color: Amber

February/March

25 Monday
3rd ♎︎
☽ v/c 8:35 am
☽ enters ♏︎ 1:05 pm
Color: White

26 Tuesday
3rd ♏︎
Color: Black

Early worshipers of Vesta buried the ashes
of their dead in small clay replicas of their homes,
which were round, thatched huts

27 Wednesday
3rd ♏︎
☽ v/c 9:53 am
Color: Topaz

Pope John XXII issues first papal bull
to discuss the practice of witchcraft, 1318

Birthday of Rudolf Steiner,
philosopher and father of the
biodynamic farming movement, 1861

◑ Thursday
3rd ♏︎
☽ enters ♐︎ 1:22 am
4th quarter 9:18 pm
Color: Crimson

29 Friday
4th ♐︎
Color: Rose

Leap Day

Set in Eastern Standard Time (EST)

1 Saturday

4th ✗

☽ v/c 11:54 am

☽ enters ♑ 1:33 pm

Color: Indigo

Preliminary hearings in the
Salem Witch trials held, 1692
Birthday of the Golden Dawn, 1888
Covenant of the Goddess (COG) formed, 1975

2 Sunday

4th ♑

Color: Yellow

If you are bothered by the energy fields of others,
try carrying peridot somewhere on your person

March

3 Monday

4th ♑
☽ v/c 1:16 am
☿ enters ♈ 9:21 pm
☽ enters ♒ 11:24 pm
Color: Lavender

*If you find your home life feeling chaotic
and out of control, clean your altar,
taking off as many items as you can*

4 Tuesday

4th ♒
♂ enters ♋ 5:01 am
Color: Maroon

Church of All Worlds incorporates in
Missouri, 1968, becoming the first Pagan
church to incorporate in the United States.

5 Wednesday

4th ♒
☽ v/c 4:46 pm
Color: Yellow

6 Thursday

4th ♒
☽ enters ♓ 5:53 am
Color: Green

Birthday of Laurie Cabot, Wiccan author

☽ Friday

4th ♓
New Moon 12:14 pm
☽ v/c 2:04 pm
Color: Purple

William Butler Yeats initiated
into the Isis-Urania Temple
of the Golden Dawn, 1890

Set in Eastern Standard Time (EST)

The Watchtower of the East

East opens the day at dawn,
Releasing the Sun
From night's ebony box.
The mind awakes
With childlike delight.
Spring fills the breeze
With sweet flowers and the
Shimmery sound of bells.
Here the birds unfurl their wings
And all the world takes flight.
                    —Elizabeth Barrette

8 Saturday

1st ♓
☽ enters ♈ 9:23 am
Color: Brown

If you wish to attract a house fairy,
keep your house neat as a pin and leave
offerings of honey, milk, and sweet butter

9 Sunday

1st ♈
Color: Gold

Daylight Saving Time begins at 2 am

March

10 Monday
1st ♈
☽ v/c 7:09 am
☽ enters ♉ 12:13 pm
Color: Ivory

Date recorded for first meeting of
Dr. John Dee and Edward Kelley, 1582

Dutch clairvoyant and psychic
healer Gerard Croiser born, 1909

11 Tuesday
1st ♉
Color: Gray

12 Wednesday
1st ♉
☽ v/c 1:26 pm
☽ enters ♊ 1:54 pm
♀ enters ♓ 6:51 pm
Color: White

Stewart Edward White, psychic
researcher, born, 1873; he later
became president of the
American Society for Psychical
Research in San Francisco

13 Thursday
1st ♊
Color: Purple

*If you're suffering creative blocks,
try using red, blue, and yellow candles together*

◐ Friday
1st ♊
2nd quarter 6:45 am
☽ v/c 4:23 pm
☽ enters ♋ 4:37 pm
☿ enters ♓ 6:46 pm
Color: Coral

Spring Equinox Easy Truffles

½ cup of margarine or butter
⅓ cup cocoa powder
¾ cup powdered sugar
Chopped nuts or coconut

Cream margarine or butter. Sift in the cocoa; make sure there are no lumps. Add powdered sugar, make sure there are no lumps there, either. Cream mixture. If the mixture is too soft, add more sugar.

Shape into a log and roll exterior in nuts or coconut. Chill for 45 minutes, then cut into slices.

Equinox is a time for celebration of life and new growth. These truffles are delicious, easy, and decadent, and can be made into round egg shapes if you like. Nurture yourself and your circle this season.

—Dallas Jennifer Cobb

15 Saturday

2nd ♋
Color: Blue

Pete Pathfinder Davis becomes the first
Wiccan priest elected as president of the
Interfaith Council of Washington State, 1995

16 Sunday

2nd ♋
☽ v/c 2:58 pm
☽ enters ♌ 9:04 pm
Color: Orange

Palm Sunday

March

17 Monday
2nd ♌
Color: Silver

St. Patrick's Day
Eleanor Shaw and Mary Phillips executed in
England for bewitching a woman
and her two children, 1705

18 Tuesday
2nd ♌
☽ v/c 2:38 pm
Color: Black

Celtic Tree Month of Alder begins
Birthday of Edgar Cayce, psychic researcher, 1877

19 Wednesday
2nd ♌
☽ enters ♍ 3:25 am
Color: Brown

Elizabethan statute against witchcraft enacted,
1563; this statute was replaced in 1604 by a
stricter one from King James I

20 Thursday
2nd ♍
☉ enters ♈ 1:48 am
☽ v/c 3:28 pm
Color: Turquoise

Ostara/Spring Equinox
Sun enters Aries
International Astrology Day
Death of Lady Sheba, Wiccan author
of *The Book of Shadows*, 2002

☺ Friday
2nd ♍
☽ enters ♎ 11:45 am
Full Moon 2:40 pm
Color: Pink

Purim
Good Friday
Storm Moon
Mandate of Henry VIII against witchcraft
enacted, 1542; repealed in 1547
Green Egg magazine founded, 1968

Libra Moon

With this Full Moon nearly at the Vernal Equinox, and the final aspect of Moon trine Neptune, this is a great time to celebrate the forces of nature. With the Moon in Libra, this is also a very good time for divination. Any workings of an air nature not meant to produce mundane effects are also appropriate.

A ritual involving music (often associated with air) would be excellent. If you play a musical instrument, especially a wind instrument, incorporate that into a Full Moon ritual. Cast a circle, and play a piece of music that you find particularly inspiring and lunar. If you prefer, bring a CD or MP3 player into your ritual, and play appropriate music. Slow, mysterious, even discordant music that you particularly enjoy would be fitting. Flute music is especially suitable because it is a quintessential air instrument. Cast a circle, start the player, and meditate on the music. Feel the music; let yourself become the music. Observe what images come to your mind as you listen. When the music is over, close the circle. If you are playing music on an instrument, you could dedicate the music to the element of air, to the Moon, or to a specific Moon deity.

—Magenta Griffith

22 Saturday
3rd ♎
Color: Gray

Pope Clement urged by Phillip IV
to suppress Templar order, 1311

23 Sunday
3rd ♎
☽ v/c 8:41 am
☽ enters ♏ 10:06 pm
Color: Amber

Easter

March

24 Monday
3rd ♏
Color: Gray

Birthday of Alyson Hannigan, who played
Willow on *Buffy the Vampire Slayer*

Arrest of Florence Newton, one of the few
Witches burned in Ireland, 1661

25 Tuesday
3rd ♏
☽ v/c 8:36 pm
Color: Red

Pope Innocent III issues papal bull to
establish the Inquisition, 1199

26 Wednesday
3rd ♏
☽ enters ♐ 10:11 am
Color: Topaz

Birthday of Joseph Campbell, author
and professor of mythology, 1910

27 Thursday
3rd ♐
Color: Crimson

28 Friday
3rd ♐
☽ v/c 9:21 am
☽ enters ♑ 10:43 pm
Color: White

Scott Cunningham dies of
complications caused by AIDS, 1993

Ostara

Ostara brings an optimistic energy as we celebrate the beginning of spring and a turning point as the Northern Hemisphere once again tilts back toward the Sun. Until this tilt takes place, now is a time of balance—equal day and night—yet also a time of anticipation, as from this night forward, the light once again conquers the darkness. Celebrate spring with the quintessential symbol of rebirth: the egg. Traditionally, Ostara or Eostre, the Teutonic goddess of spring and dawn, was represented with fertile rabbits at her feet. At this time, plant life becomes greener and increasingly abundant, trees and flowers pollinate, and animals emerge from their winter hibernation.

Consider a short fast, or a day or two of detoxification. After a winter of eating rich foods, our bodies often build up toxins. To cleanse, drink herbal teas and spring water, and eat fresh fruits, vegetables, and nuts. Avoid sugar, dairy, caffeine, red meats, and processed foods. You will feel lighter and have more energy. Decorate a hard-boiled egg with symbols that represent your dreams and goals. Bury your egg in your garden to hatch your wishes.

—Emely Flak

☽ Saturday

3rd ♑
♀ enters ♊ 5:21 am
4th quarter 5:47 pm
Color: Black

30 Sunday
4th ♑
Color: Orange

A necklace of poppy seeds protects infants from the evil eye

March/April

31 Monday

4th ♑
☽ v/c 12:54 am
☽ enters ♒ 9:34 am
Color: Lavender

Last Witch trial in Ireland,
held at Magee Island, 1711

1 Tuesday

4th ♒
Color: White

April Fools' Day (All Fools' Day—Pagan)

2 Wednesday

4th ♒
☽ v/c 5:13 am
♇ ℞ 5:23 am
☿ enters ♈ 1:44 pm
☽ enters ♓ 4:55 pm
Color: Brown

*Try growing a parsley plant in your kitchen
for both cooking and to "recycle" negative energy;
just make sure you provide it with a deep pot*

3 Thursday

4th ♓
Color: Green

4 Friday

4th ♓
☽ v/c 5:43 pm
☽ enters ♈ 8:27 pm
Color: Pink

*Don't change the bed clothes on a Friday
unless you want to have bad dreams*

Set in Eastern Daylight Time (EDT)

☽ Saturday

4th ♈

New Moon 11:55 pm

Color: Blue

Trial of Alice Samuel, her
husband, and her daughter, who
were accused of bewitching the
wife of Sir Henry Cromwell and
several village children, 1593

6 Sunday

1st ♈

♀ enters ♈ 1:35 am

☽ v/c 11:01 am

☽ enters ♉ 9:19 pm

Color: Yellow

April

7 Monday
1st ♉
Color: Gray

Church of All Worlds founded, 1962
First Wiccan "tract" published
by Pete Pathfinder Davis, 1996

8 Tuesday
1st ♉
☽ v/c 11:12 am
☽ enters ♊ 9:27 pm
Color: Black

William Alexander Aynton initiated into
the Isis-Urania temple of the Golden
Dawn, 1896; he would later be called the
"Grand Old Man" of the Golden Dawn

9 Wednesday
1st ♊
Color: Yellow

10 Thursday
1st ♊
☽ v/c 12:11 pm
☽ enters ♋ 10:43 pm
Color: Turquoise

Birthday of Rev. Montague Summers,
orthodox scholar and author of
A History of Witchcraft and Demonology, 1880

11 Friday
1st ♋
Color: White

Burning of Major Weir, Scottish "sorcerer"
who confessed of his own accord, 1670;
some historians believe that the major
became delusional or senile because up
until his confession he had an excellent
reputation and was a pillar of society

The Maiden Goddess

The Maiden dances, pale and fair,
On April mornings soft with rain
With apple blossoms in Her hair
And green leaves trailing from Her train.

In pastures thick with silver dew
She stops to bless each calf and cow.
Her duty here is to renew,
A waxing crescent on Her brow.

She sows the seeds of things to come
As fresh and innocent as air
But in the distance, summer's drum
Will beckon Her from here to there.
                    —Elizabeth Barrette

○ Saturday
1st ♋
2nd quarter 2:32 pm
☽ v/c 2:32 pm
Color: Indigo

There is a Japanese belief that if a cat
grows old enough, it can become
a shape-shifter called a bake neko

13 Sunday
2nd ♋
☽ enters ♌ 2:29 am
Color: Amber

April

14 Monday
2nd ♌
Color: Lavender

Adoption of the Principles of
Wiccan Belief at "Witch Meet"
in St. Paul, Minnesota, 1974

15 Tuesday
2nd ♌
☽ v/c 12:56 am
☽ enters ♍ 9:06 am
Color: Gray

Celtic Tree Month of Willow begins

Birthday of Elizabeth Montgomery,
who played Samantha on *Bewitched*, 1933

16 Wednesday
2nd ♍
Color: White

Birthday of Margot Adler, author
of *Drawing Down the Moon*

17 Thursday
2nd ♍
☽ v/c 1:59 am
☿ enters ♉ 5:07 pm
☽ enters ♎ 6:10 pm
Color: Purple

Aleister Crowley breaks into and takes over the
Golden Dawn temple, providing the catalyst for
the demise of the original Golden Dawn, 1900

18 Friday
2nd ♎
⚹ ℞ 8:48 am
Color: Rose

Scorpio Moon

This Scorpio Full Moon is less useful than next month's. Moon square Neptune as a final aspect is awkward, with Neptune's tendency toward illusion and delusion. Despite the Scorpio nature of this Moon, love magic is likely to backfire. Instead, self-examination aimed at discovering and ending self-delusion and self-sabotage would be more useful. This is a good time to dispel any deception and misunderstanding.

Spell to disperse delusion: Find a thin piece of cloth that is easy to tear. You need at least enough cloth to veil your face. Find a comfortable-fitting hat with a brim in front. Sew or pin the fabric to the hat so it hangs down in front. Wear this veiled hat as you begin this ritual.

Cast your circle as usual. If the veil gets in the way, pull it up and over your head. Once the circle is cast, pull it down again. Chant "Dispel illusion, disappear like smoke," or write your own words to recite, over and over, faster and faster. When you feel the energy peak, rip the veil in two up the middle. Shout, "Illusion begone! So mote it be!" Close the circle, being careful to ground and disperse all the energy.

—Magenta Griffith

19 Saturday

2nd ♎
⚷ enters ♈ 4:07 am
☉ enters ♉ 12:51 pm
☽ v/c 4:54 pm
Color: Black

Sun enters Taurus
Conviction of Witches
at second of four famous trials at
Chelmsford, England, 1579

☺ Sunday

2nd ♎
☽ enters ♏ 5:00 am
Full Moon 6:25 am
Color: Gold

Passover begins
Wind Moon

April

21 Monday
3rd ♏︎
Color: White

*The Persian Baal Festival took place on April 21
and may have been the model for Ireland's Beltane*

22 Tuesday
3rd ♏︎
☽ v/c 4:53 am
☽ enters ♐︎ 5:07 pm
Color: Red

Earth Day; the first Earth Day was in 1970

23 Wednesday
3rd ♐︎
Color: Topaz

Edward III of England begins the
Order of the Garter, 1350
First National All-Woman Conference on
Women's Spirituality held, Boston, 1976

24 Thursday
3rd ♐︎
☽ v/c 5:37 pm
Color: White

25 Friday
3rd ♐︎
☽ enters ♑︎ 5:47 am
Color: Coral

Orthodox Good Friday
USA Today reports that Patricia Hutchins
is the first military Wiccan granted
religious leave for the sabbats, 1989

Beltane Passion Cookies

¾ cup margarine or unsalted butter
1 cup brown sugar
⅛ cup silken tofu or one egg
¼ cup molasses
1¾ cups whole grain flour
½ tsp. salt
3 tsps. ground cinnamon
1½ tsps. ground cloves
5 tsps. powdered ginger
⅛ cup granulated sugar
2 tsps. baking soda
½ cup crystallized ginger, coarsely
   chopped (optional)

Preheat the oven to 350 degrees F. Line a cookie sheet with parchment paper. Using a hand mixer, cream the margarine or butter with the sugar, then beat in tofu or egg and molasses. Sift all the dry ingredients into a medium bowl, then stir into wet batter. Add crystallized ginger.

Roll batter into 1-inch balls, and dip one side in granulated sugar. Place sugar-side up on baking sheet, about 3 inches apart. Bake 10 to 12 minutes. Cool on wire rack. These cookies will awaken your passions after the long cool sleep of winter. Share them with your lover, or eat them alone.

—Dallas Jennifer Cobb

26 Saturday

3rd ♑
Color: Gray

Children who died in April were
believed to have been carried off by the
fairies, who loved them for their beauty

27 Sunday

3rd ♑
☽ v/c 10:18 am
☽ enters ♒ 5:27 pm
Color: Orange

Orthodox Easter
Passover ends

April/May

☽ Monday

3rd ≈
4th quarter 10:12 am
Color: Silver

Divination on May Eve using yarrow
allows a young girl to dream of her future

29 Tuesday

4th ≈
Color: Scarlet

Birthday of Ed Fitch, Wiccan author

30 Wednesday

4th ≈
☽ v/c 1:25 am
☽ enters ♓ 2:11 am
♀ enters ♉ 9:34 am
Color: Brown

Walpurgis Night; traditionally the
German Witches gather on the Blocksberg,
a mountain in northeastern Germany

1 Thursday

4th ♓
Color: Purple

Beltane/May Day
Order of the Illuminati formed in
Bavaria by Adam Weishaupt, 1776

2 Friday

4th ♓
☽ v/c 5:34 am
☽ enters ♈ 6:51 am
☿ enters ♊ 4:00 pm
♄ D 11:07 pm
Color: White

Birthday of D. J. Conway, Wiccan author

Set in Eastern Daylight Time (EDT)

Beltane

Beltane is the sensual Pagan festival of fire and fertility, and is also known as May Day—when we dance around the omnipotent phallic symbol, the maypole. The red and white ribbons woven around the maypole represent blood and semen; the sacred fusion of female and male energies that are the creative life force.

Capture the essence of this potent fertility celebration by weaving or plaiting red and white cord or ribbon. Leave some loose, unplaited ribbon at the end to cut later. Wear your woven cord as a headdress or place onto your altar in a heart shape. Head wreaths were traditionally worn at Beltane to honor the Queen of May.

If you are single, to attract a partner, grab a red pen and a piece of white paper and write the qualities you admire in a lover. If you are in a relationship, list what you enjoy about your partner, plus a few traits you may wish to nurture. Then add what you love about yourself. Roll up the piece of paper and tie with the leftover red and white ribbon. Place it under your pillow as you sleep tonight, thinking about the joy your partner, or potential partner, will bring. When you wake, store the scroll of paper in a safe place.

—Emely Flak

3 Saturday
4th ♈
Color: Black

4 Sunday
4th ♈
☽ v/c 3:16 am
☽ enters ♉ 7:58 am
Color: Yellow

The *New York Herald Tribune* carries the story of a woman who brought her neighbor to court on a charge of bewitchment, 1895

May

☽ Monday
4th ♉
New Moon 8:18 am
Color: Ivory

Cinco de Mayo
Beltane crossquarter day
(Sun reaches 15° Taurus)

6 Tuesday
1st ♉
☽ v/c 4:21 am
☽ enters ♊ 7:17 am
Color: Scarlet

Long Island Church of Aphrodite
formed by Reverend Gleb Botkin, 1938

7 Wednesday
1st ♊
☽ v/c 9:36 pm
Color: Brown

8 Thursday
1st ♊
☽ enters ♋ 7:02 am
Color: Turquoise

Amber is a good stone for grounding

9 Friday
1st ♋
♃ ℞ 8:11 am
♂ enters ♌ 4:20 pm
☽ v/c 8:06 pm
Color: Rose

Joan of Arc canonized, 1920
First day of the Lemuria, a Roman
festival of the dead; this festival
was probably borrowed from the
Etruscans and is one possible
ancestor of our modern Halloween

10 Saturday
1st ♋
☽ enters ♌ 9:10 am
Color: Blue

☽ Sunday
1st ♌
2nd quarter 11:47 pm
Color: Orange

Mother's Day
Massachusetts Bay Colony Puritans
ban Christmas celebrations
because they are too Pagan, 1659

May

12 Monday
2nd ♌
☽ v/c 4:09 am
☽ enters ♍ 2:48 pm
Color: Silver

13 Tuesday
2nd ♍
Color: Gray

Celtic Tree Month of Hawthorn begins

14 Wednesday
2nd ♍
☽ v/c 12:38 pm
☽ enters ♎ 11:46 pm
Color: Topaz

Widow Robinson of Kidderminster
and her two daughters are arrested for
trying to prevent the return of Charles II
from exile by use of magic, 1660

15 Thursday
2nd ♎
Color: White

16 Friday
2nd ♎
☽ v/c 11:29 pm
Color: Coral

An Egyptian's Chief Wife was the actual
ruler of the household and legal owner of the
household possessions and furniture

Set in Eastern Daylight Time (EDT)

The Athame

Athame is a two-edged blade
Of metal and of magic made

It turns all hostile magic back
With shining steel and handle black

When ways are closed,
*   it cuts right through*
And all that binds, it severs, too

Upon the hilt, a Witch's name
To second-sight burns bright with flame

And only to that hand, this blade
Will serve and answer as it's bade
                              —Elizabeth Barrette

17 Saturday

2nd ♎
☽ enters ♏ 10:59 am
Color: Indigo

In dreams, dungeons contain
those things we wish to lock away

18 Sunday

2nd ♏
Color: Amber

The color green helps reduce fatigue

May

☺ Monday
2nd ♏
☽ v/c 10:11 pm
Full Moon 10:11 pm
☽ enters ♐ 11:18 pm
Color: Lavender

Flower Moon

20 Tuesday
3rd ♐
♀ enters ♉ 9:54 am
☉ enters ♊ 12:01 pm
Color: Red

Sun enters Gemini

21 Wednesday
3rd ♐
Color: White

Birthday of Gwyddion Pendderwen,
Pagan bard, 1946

22 Thursday
3rd ♐
☽ v/c 12:19 am
☽ enters ♑ 11:55 am
Color: Green

Adoption of the Earth Religion
Anti-Abuse Act, 1988

23 Friday
3rd ♑
Color: Pink

Set in Eastern Daylight Time (EDT)

Scorpio Moon Redux

We get an extra Full Moon in Scorpio this year. This month is excellent for magic working—especially love magic. If you have a partner, a two-person ritual to strengthen the relationship could be helpful and fun. The Full Moon, Sun opposite Moon, is the final aspect. Oppositions are about balance and harmony, so a ritual involving balancing polarities would work well: masculine and feminine, earth and sky, mind and body. If you don't have a partner, you can work on balancing forces within yourself.

Find a large mirror you can bring into the circle, or do the ritual near a large mirror. Cast a circle with the mirror in the center. If the mirror is on the wall, visualize the circle extending to the other side of the mirror.

Look at yourself in the mirror. Reach out and place your palms on the mirror like you are holding hands with yourself. Feel energy flow in yourself, through the mirror, and back to you. Notice all the contradictions within yourself, the opposites that we all contain. After a few minutes, let the energy slow to a halt, and break contact with the image in the mirror. Close the circle. Your might want to record any dreams you have after this ritual.

—Magenta Griffith

24 Saturday

3rd ♑
☽ v/c 8:26 am
♀ enters ♊ 6:52 pm
☽ enters ♒ 11:51 pm
Color: Gray

The fifth day after the Full Moon
is usually considered fertile

25 Sunday

3rd ♒
⚷ ℞ 7:42 am
Color: Gold

Scott Cunningham initiated into
the Traditional Gwyddonic
Order of the Wicca, 1981

May/June

26 Monday

3rd ≈
☿ ℞ 11:48 am
♆ ℞ 12:14 pm
☽ v/c 10:49 pm
Color: White

Memorial Day (observed)

○ Tuesday

3rd ≈
☽ enters ♓ 9:38 am
4th quarter 10:56 pm
Color: Black

Birthday of Morning Glory
Zell-Ravenheart, Church of All Worlds

Final confession of witchcraft by
Isobel Gowdie, Scotland, 1662

28 Wednesday

4th ♓
Color: Yellow

Listed as the original patent holders
for the Ouija, or talking board, was inventor
Elijah Bond and two business associates

29 Thursday

4th ♓
☽ v/c 2:23 am
☽ enters ♈ 3:52 pm
Color: Crimson

30 Friday

4th ♈
Color: Purple

Death of Joan of Arc, 1431

The Mother Goddess

The Mother works beneath a tree
All through the sultry afternoon
A basket heavy at Her knee
As She picks peaches sweet as June.

She loves Her labor, branch and root,
And blesses honest sweat that flows.
As ripe and rich as any fruit,
The full moon in Her belly grows.

Her arms are strong, Her
     hands are brown.
What She creates is bright with life.
No mortal queen wore finer crown . . .
But yonder winter hones its knife.
                    —Elizabeth Barrette

31 Saturday
4th ♈
☽ v/c 8:54 am
☽ enters ♉ 6:18 pm
Color: Indigo

To dream of a fountain means that
something new is coming to your notice

1 Sunday
4th ♉
Color: Yellow

Witchcraft Act of 1563
takes effect in England

June

2 Monday

4th ♉
☽ v/c 9:02 am
☽ enters ♊ 6:06 pm
Color: Gray

Birthday of Alessandro
di Cagliostro, magician, 1743

☽ Tuesday

4th ♊
New Moon 3:22 pm
Color: Red

4 Wednesday

1st ♊
☽ v/c 8:08 am
☽ enters ♋ 5:16 pm
Color: Yellow

An abalone or scallop shell would make a
great water holder on a small altar dedicated
to love or the element of water

5 Thursday

1st ♋
Color: Green

Burn blue and white candles together for luck

6 Friday

1st ♋
☽ v/c 5:32 am
☽ enters ♌ 6:00 pm
Color: White

Set in Eastern Daylight Time (EDT)

7 Saturday

1st ♌
Color: Brown

8 Sunday

1st ♌
☽ v/c 11:40 am
☽ enters ♍ 10:01 pm
Color: Orange

*In Chinese mythology, the Moon
is a place where the immortals and
fairies live, rather than a living deity*

June

9 Monday
1st ♍
Color: Lavender

Shavuot
Birthday of Grace Cook, medium and
founder of the White Eagle Lodge, 1892

◑ Tuesday
1st ♍
2nd quarter 11:03 am
☽ v/c 3:42 pm
Color: White

Celtic Tree Month of Oak begins
Hanging of Bridget Bishop, first to
die in the Salem Witch trials, 1692

11 Wednesday
2nd ♍
☽ enters ♎ 5:55 am
♀ enters ♋ 11:56 am
Color: Brown

12 Thursday
2nd ♎
Color: Turquoise

13 Friday
2nd ♎
☽ v/c 5:15 am
☽ enters ♏ 4:53 pm
Color: Pink

Birthday of William Butler Yeats, poet and
member of the Golden Dawn, 1865
Birthday of Gerald Gardner, founder
of the Gardnerian tradition, 1884

Set in Eastern Daylight Time (EDT)

Celebration Slush

1 ripe banana
1 cup frozen strawberries
1 tsp. flaxseed
⅓ cup soymilk or cow's milk

Put all ingredients in a blender or food processor, and puree. If the slush is too thick for you, add a little more soymilk. Scoop into bowls and enjoy. Makes four servings.

   The longest day of the year arrives at peak strawberry season. So enjoy the bounty of the earth with this sinful, simple, and succulent slush. Just when you thought there was nothing decadent that was really good for you . . .

—Dallas Jennifer Cobb

14 Saturday

2nd ♏
♇ enters ♐ 1:13 am
Color: Gray

Flag Day

15 Sunday

2nd ♏
☽ v/c 5:29 pm
Color: Gold

Father's Day
Margaret Jones becomes the first person executed as a Witch in the Massachusetts Bay Colony, 1648; she was a Boston doctor who was accused of witchcraft after several of her patients died

June

16 Monday
2nd ♏
☽ enters ♐ 5:19 am
Color: White

Three butterflies together mean good luck

17 Tuesday
2nd ♐
Color: Black

Birthday of Starhawk, Wiccan author

☺ Wednesday
2nd ♐
♀ enters ♋ 4:48 am
Full Moon 1:30 pm
☽ v/c 5:37 pm
☽ enters ♑ 5:51 pm
Color: White

Strong Sun Moon
Church of All Worlds
chartered with the IRS, 1970

19 Thursday
3rd ♑
☿ D 10:31 am
Color: Purple

20 Friday
3rd ♑
☽ v/c 3:02 pm
☉ enters ♋ 7:59 pm
Color: Rose

Midsummer/Litha/Summer Solstice
Sun enters Cancer

Set in Eastern Daylight Time (EDT)

Sagittarius Moon

With Pluto and the Full Moon in the same degree as a final aspect, this is an excellent time to bring new influences into your life. The Moon goes void-of-course four hours after the Full Moon, so time the ritual accordingly. Sagittarius is the sign associated with the vast scope of the universe, grasping the big picture, expansiveness. Step out of your ruts, expand your point of view, study something new, or embark on a new path.

Rather than a formal ritual, plan a small, symbolic amount of work at the exact moment of Full Moon. Start a book on the study of Qabala, astrology, or any subject you've been meaning to get around to. Start that new project, even if that just means laying out the pattern for a new robe or beginning to sand a new wand. If retail stores are open at the Full Moon, consider shopping for materials for your new magical project or technique.

Since one characteristic of Sagittarius is biting off more than you can chew, be careful to pick a realistic project. Plan to read one book, not a dozen. If you go shopping, consider your finances carefully. Be realistic about how much time, money, and energy you can devote to your new endeavor.

—Magenta Griffith

21 Saturday

3rd ♑
☽ enters ♒ 5:33 am
Color: Blue

22 Sunday

3rd ♒
Color: Amber

Final witchcraft law in
England repealed, 1951

June

23 Monday

3rd ≈
☽ v/c 3:04 pm
☽ enters ♓ 3:32 pm
Color: Silver

24 Tuesday

3rd ♓
Color: Gray

Birthday of Janet Farrar, Wiccan author

James I Witchcraft Statute of 1604 is
replaced in 1763 with a law against
pretending to practice divination and
witchcraft; law stands until 1951

25 Wednesday

3rd ♓
☽ v/c 10:16 pm
☽ enters ♈ 10:49 pm
Color: Topaz

A law is introduced in Germany by
Archbishop Siegfried III to encourage
conversion rather than burning of heretics, 1233

◑ Thursday

3rd ♈
4th quarter 8:10 am
♅ ℞ 8:01 pm
Color: White

Birthday of Stewart Farrar, Wiccan author

Richard of Gloucester assumes the English
throne after accusing the widowed
queen of Edward IV of witchcraft, 1483

27 Friday

4th ♈
Color: Purple

Birthday of Scott Cunningham,
Wiccan author, 1956

Set in Eastern Daylight Time (EDT)

Summer Solstice

When the Sun is at its peak in the sky at our Summer Solstice, Earth is as close as possible to the Sun. Litha is the ancient Germanic name for summer and the time to celebrate its warmth. This important time in the solar year is when the Oak King, God of Light, hands over reign to the Holly King, God of Darkness, who rules from this point forward for the other half of the year.

At this time when light will begin to wane, decorate you altar and house with sunflowers. Place honey on your altar to represent life's sweetness. Light the same gold candle for a short time for four or five nights over this period. On the last evening, after the candle is safely snuffed, wrap what is left of it in yellow or gold colored cloth with sunflower seeds. Tie the parcel with a yellow ribbon and keep it somewhere safe for protection and good fortune until next Litha.

Make a sunflower solstice cake decorated with yellow icing and sunflower seeds to share with your friends over a glass of mead. Enjoy time outdoors, allowing the Sun to warm your body as you relax, walk, or read. Bid farewell to the Sun god for a few months and be assured, he will return.

—Emely Flak

28 Saturday
4th ♈
☽ v/c 2:14 am
☽ enters ♉ 2:50 am
Color: Indigo

29 Sunday
4th ♉
Color: Yellow

*Some consider daisies to be the spirits
of children who died at birth*

June/July

30 Monday

4th ♉
⚷ enters ♉ 12:56 am
☽ v/c 2:43 am
☽ enters ♊ 4:03 am
Color: Ivory

Marry in July and you'll live to sigh

1 Tuesday

4th ♊
♂ enters ♍ 12:21 pm
Color: Scarlet

☽ Wednesday

4th ♊
☽ v/c 3:08 am
☽ enters ♋ 3:53 am
New Moon 10:18 pm
Color: Yellow

3 Thursday

1st ♋
☽ v/c 4:13 pm
Color: Turquoise

Trial of Joan Prentice, who was accused
of sending an imp in the form of a
ferret to bite children; she allegedly had
two imps named Jack and Jill, 1549

4 Friday
1st ♋
☽ enters ♌ 4:15 am
Color: Coral

Independence Day

5 Saturday

1st ♌
Color: Blue

Conviction of Witches at third of four
famous trials at Chelmsford, England, 1589

6 Sunday

1st ♌
☽ v/c 6:04 am
☽ enters ♍ 7:04 am
Color: Orange

Scott Cunningham is initiated into
the Ancient Pictish Gaelic Way, 1981

July

7 Monday

1st ♍
Color: Gray

8 Tuesday

1st ♍
☽ v/c 12:21 pm
☽ enters ♎ 1:31 pm
Color: White

Celtic Tree Month of Holly begins

9 Wednesday

1st ♎
Color: Brown

Death of Herman Slater,
proprietor of Magickal Childe
bookstore in New York, 1992
Birthday of Amber K, Wiccan author

◐ Thursday

1st ♎
2nd quarter 12:35 am
☿ enters ♋ 4:17 pm
☽ v/c 10:14 pm
☽ enters ♏ 11:35 pm
Color: Green

11 Friday

2nd ♏
Color: Pink

The Etruscans had a lasting influence on what became the Roman Empire, as gathered from the names of the most powerful triune of deities: Uni (Juno), Minrva (Minerva), and Tinia (Jupiter)

82   *Set in Eastern Daylight Time (EDT)*

The Watchtower of the South

South is the Sun's fire
In the fierce forge of noon,
Beating the soul into shape.
Young blood burns
With the heat of summer.
Hearts pound in passion.
This is the place
Where the lion waits,
Tawny with promise,
To pounce upon the prize.
>   —Elizabeth Barrette

12 Saturday

2nd ♏
♀ enters ♌ 2:39 pm
☽ v/c 11:05 pm
Color: Black

13 Sunday

2nd ♏
☽ enters ♐ 11:50 am
Color: Gold

Birthday of Dr. John Dee, magician, 1527

July

14 Monday
2nd ♐
Color: Silver

First crop circles recorded
on Silbury Hill, 1988

15 Tuesday
2nd ♐
☽ v/c 10:44 pm
Color: Black

Carry some black peppercorns with you
when in need of extra courage

16 Wednesday
2nd ♐
☽ enters ♑ 12:20 am
Color: White

17 Thursday
2nd ♑
Color: Purple

First airing of *The Witching Hour*, a
Pagan radio show hosted by Winter
Wren and Don Lewis, on station
WONX in Evanston, Illinois, 1992

☺ Friday
2nd ♑
Full Moon 3:59 am
☽ v/c 3:59 am
☽ enters ♒ 11:40 am
Color: Rose

Blessing Moon

Set in Eastern Daylight Time (EDT)

Capricorn Moon

The Full Moon itself is the final aspect this month, and with Moon in Capricorn, this is a classic time to balance energies on the material plane and the mystical. If you have tools you wish to consecrate, here is a simple ritual.

You will need physical representations of the elements: a candle for fire, a small bowl of water, a stick of incense in a holder (or an incense burner with charcoal). For earth, you may use salt, dirt, or a stone. With the tools/items you wish to consecrate on the altar or elsewhere, cast a circle, and invoke your usual goddesses or gods. Take the tool or object, pass it carefully above the flame of the candle, and say, "I consecrate this (wand, tool) by fire." Then sprinkle a few drops of water on it and say "I consecrate this by water." Pass the object through the smoke from the incense burner and say, "I consecrate this by air." Finally, touch the object to the salt or dirt and say, "I consecrate this by earth." Then raise it above your head and say, "I consecrate this to the service of the gods (or goddess, etc.). Then close your circle, and put your newly consecrated tool on your altar, or in a safe place.

—Magenta Griffith

19 Saturday

3rd ≈
Color: Brown

Rebecca Nurse hanged in
Salem, Massachusetts, 1692

20 Sunday

3rd ≈
☽ v/c 7:25 pm
☽ enters ♓ 9:07 pm
Color: Yellow

Pope Adrian VI issues a papal bull to the
Inquisition to re-emphasize the 1503
bull of Julius II calling for the purging
of "sorcerers by fire and sword," 1523

July

21 Monday
3rd ♓
Color: Lavender

22 Tuesday
3rd ♓
☉ enters ♌ 6:55 am
Color: Gray

Sun Enters Leo
Northamptonshire Witches
condemned, 1612
First modern recorded sighting
of the Loch Ness Monster, 1930

23 Wednesday
3rd ♓
☽ v/c 2:39 am
☽ enters ♈ 4:22 am
Color: Topaz

Lughnasadh was a feast to commemorate the
funeral games of Tailtiu, Lugh's foster mother

24 Thursday
3rd ♈
Color: White

☽ Friday
3rd ♈
☽ v/c 7:30 am
☽ enters ♉ 9:14 am
4th quarter 2:41 pm
Color: Purple

Death of Pope Innocent VIII, who issued
bull *Summis Desiderantes Affectibus*, 1492

Set in Eastern Daylight Time (EDT)

Lammas Latkes

2 lbs. new potatoes, grated
2 T. olive oil
1 medium red onion, finely chopped
¼ cup whole grain flour
1 tsp. salt
¼ tsp. pepper
¼ cup silken tofu or 2 eggs

Heat oven to 450 degrees F. Grate potatoes, add all other ingredients, and mix well. Drop large tablespoons of the mixture onto a cookie sheet. Bake for 10 minutes, turn, then bake for 5 minutes. Serve with apple sauce or sour cream.

Celebrate the ripening time with potato latkes. If you have a garden, take the time to connect with nature and dig your own new potatoes. If not, buy some knowing they were recently nestled in the earth. As you savor these tasty snacks, remember how dependent we are on the earth and the plants that grow.

—Dallas Jennifer Cobb

26 Saturday

4th ♉
☿ enters ♌ 7:48 am
Color: Indigo

Confession of Chelmsford Witches at first of four famous trials at Chelmsford, 1566; the others were held in 1579, 1589, and 1645; "Witch Finder General" Matthew Hopkins presided at the 1645 trials

27 Sunday

4th ♉
☽ v/c 12:52 am
☽ enters ♊ 11:55 am
Color: Amber

Jennet Preston becomes the first of the "Malkin Tower" Witches to be hung; she was convicted of hiring Witches to help her murder Thomas Lister, 1612

July/August

28 Monday
4th ♊
Color: Ivory

29 Tuesday
4th ♊
☽ v/c 11:25 am
☽ enters ♋ 1:11 pm
Color: Red

Agnes Waterhouse, one of the Chelmsford Witches, is hanged under the new witchcraft statute of Elizabeth I, 1566; she was accused of having a spotted cat familiar named Sathan

30 Wednesday
4th ♋
Color: Yellow

Conrad of Marburg is murdered on the open road, presumably because he had shifted from persecuting poor heretics to nobles, 1233

31 Thursday
4th ♋
☽ v/c 1:31 am
☽ enters ♌ 2:21 pm
Color: Crimson

Birthday of H. P. Blavatsky, founder of the Theosophical Society, 1831

Date of fabled meeting of British Witches to raise cone of power to stop Hitler's invasion of England, 1940

☽ Friday
4th ♌
New Moon 6:12 am
Color: Rose

Lammas/Lughnasadh
Solar eclipse 6:22 am, 9° ♌ 32'
Birthday of Edward Kelley, medium of Dr. John Dee, 1555
AURORA Network UK founded, 2000

Set in Eastern Daylight Time (EDT)

Lughnasadh

Named after Lugh, the Celtic god of fire, Lughnasadh is also commonly recognized as the harvest celebration of Lammas. Our contemporary, urban lifestyles and ultra-modern farming methods make the significance of an abundant harvest difficult to grasp. But for our ancestors, it marked the end of summer, a time to gather corn and other crops. Food such as seeds, fruit, herbs, and grain were gathered and preserved.  Corn dollies were created to symbolize the goddess. The word "Lammas" literally translates to "loaf mass" and is said to be the Christian name for this bread festival, when bread was baked from the first corn cutting.

A bread feast is an appropriate celebratory ritual for Lammas. Gather your friends, asking each to bring a different loaf variety, which will result in an interestingly delicious experience. Try to include grainy bread, savory, fruit-infused bread, fruit-flavored breads (like banana), and vegetable-based bread (like pumpkin or zucchini). Just before your feast, place a small piece of bread on your altar and take a few moments to contemplate your gratitude for the abundance you are about to enjoy!

—Emely Flak

2 Saturday

1st ♌
☽ v/c 2:59 pm
☽ enters ♍ 4:59 pm
Color: Brown

Birthday of Henry Steele Olcott,
who cofounded the Theosophical
Society with H. P. Blavatsky, 1832

3 Sunday

1st ♍
Color: Gold

When an eclipse occurs during low sunspot activity, the
Sun's corona halo around the Moon gives the impression of
a large white bird, similar to the Egyptian winged disc symbol

August

4 Monday

1st ♍
♀ enters ♊ 3:30 am
☽ v/c 8:16 pm
☽ enters ♎ 10:28 pm
Color: Silver

Pearls used to be given to a bride in the hopes
that she would bear many children

5 Tuesday

1st ♎
Color: White

Celtic Tree Month of Hazel begins

6 Wednesday

1st ♎
♀ enters ♍ 12:20 am
Color: Yellow

7 Thursday

1st ♎
☽ v/c 5:01 am
☽ enters ♏ 7:26 am
Color: Green

Lammas crossquarter day
(Sun reaches 15° Leo)

◐ Friday

1st ♏
✳ D 5:40 am
2nd quarter 4:20 pm
Color: White

9 Saturday

2nd ♏
☽ v/c 5:02 pm
☽ enters ♐ 7:10 pm
Color: Gray

10 Sunday

2nd ♐
☿ enters ♍ 6:51 am
Color: Yellow

Carry turquoise for safety when traveling

August

11 Monday
2nd ♐
Color: White

Laurie Cabot withdraws from Salem,
Massachusetts, mayoral race, 1987
Birthday of Edain McCoy, Wiccan author

12 Tuesday
2nd ♐
☽ v/c 5:04 am
☽ enters ♑ 7:42 am
Color: Black

13 Wednesday
2nd ♑
Color: Brown

Aradia de Toscano allegedly
born in Volterra, Italy, 1313
Church of Wicca founded in Australia
by Lady Tamara Von Forslun, 1989

14 Thursday
2nd ♑
☽ v/c 1:09 pm
☽ enters ♒ 6:56 pm
Color: Turquoise

15 Friday
2nd ♒
Color: Pink

Birthday of Charles Godfrey Leland,
author of *Aradia, Gospel of Witches*, 1824

Set in Eastern Daylight Time (EDT)

Aquarius Moon

The Full Moon in Aquarius is another eclipse. The final aspect of Moon sextile Pluto is great for calling forth magical opportunities and enhancing communication with other realms.

If you have never tried trance-work, this is an auspicious time to start. Think about what you want to do in trance. Have a pen and paper handy to record the results.

Sit or lie down in a comfortable position. Allow yourself to relax completely. Then visualize yourself going down a long staircase. Count the steps as you go down. Every ten steps there is a landing where you can pause. So you go down, one, two, three steps. You find yourself becoming more relaxed. Most people find that going down three to five sets of ten steps puts them in a light trance, relaxed enough to explore parts of their mind that are usually inaccessible.

While in trance, try projecting yourself to a comfortable place, such as a beach or a mountain lake. You may meet a wise teacher or mythological figure during this experience. When you feel the experience is over, count backwards from ten to one, and then shout, "Wake up."

—Magenta Griffith

☻ Saturday

2nd ≈
Full Moon 5:16 pm
Color: Blue

Corn Moon
Lunar eclipse 5:11 pm, 24° ≈ 21'

17 Sunday

3rd ≈
☽ v/c 1:14 am
☽ enters ♓ 3:46 am
Color: Amber

Scott Cunningham's first
initiation into Wicca, 1973

August

18 Monday
3rd ♓
Color: Black

Father Urban Grandier found
guilty of bewitching nuns at a
convent in Loudoun, France, 1634

19 Tuesday
3rd ♓
♂ enters ♎ 6:03 am
☽ v/c 7:41 am
☽ enters ♈ 10:10 am
♀ enters ♌ 5:25 pm
Color: Gray

John Willard and Reverend
George Burroughs put to death
in the Salem Witch trials, 1692

20 Wednesday
3rd ♈
Color: Topaz

Execution of Lancashire Witches, 1612
Birthday of H. P. Lovecraft, horror
writer and alleged magician, 1890
Birthday of Ann Moura, author and Witch

21 Thursday
3rd ♈
☽ v/c 12:53 pm
☽ enters ♉ 7:38 pm
Color: Green

22 Friday
3rd ♉
☉ enters ♍ 2:02 pm
Color: Purple

Sun enters Virgo
Pope John XXII orders the Inquisition at
Carcassonne to seize the property of Witches, sor-
cerers, and those who make wax images, 1320

The God

The God is day, the Goddess night.
Above Her Earth, He is the sky.
Beyond Her darkness, He is light.
Where She is deep, He must be high.

He is the lightning and the Sun.
In sacrifice His power lies,
And in the antlered stags that run
The glory lives of all that dies.

Male to Her female, He is drawn;
Projecting all that She receives.
With secret smile He looks on,
A hidden face in forest leaves.
                    —Elizabeth Barrette

◑ Saturday

3rd ♉
☽ v/c 5:19 am
☽ enters ♊ 5:48 pm
4th quarter 7:49 pm
Color: Black

24 Sunday

4th ♊
Color: Orange

A primrose is extremely protective,
provided you pick it before sunrise

August

25 Monday

4th ♊
☽ v/c 5:52 pm
☽ enters ♋ 8:18 pm
Color: Lavender

One wise counsel is worth the strength of many

26 Tuesday
4th ♋
Color: Scarlet

27 Wednesday
4th ♋
☽ v/c 8:13 pm
☽ enters ♌ 10:51 pm
Color: Yellow

28 Thursday

4th ♌
☿ enters ♎ 10:50 pm
Color: Purple

29 Friday

4th ♌
☽ v/c 11:44 pm
Color: Coral

Election of Pope Innocent VIII, who issued the
papal bull *Summis Desiderantes Affectibus*, 1484

Set in Eastern Daylight Time (EDT)

☽ Saturday
1th ♌
☽ enters ♍ 2:18 am
♀ enters ♎ 10:41 am
New Moon 3:58 pm
Color: Indigo

31 Sunday
1st ♍
Color: Gold

Birthday of Raymond Buckland,
who, along with his wife, Rosemary,
is generally credited with bringing
Gardnerian Wicca to the United States

September

1 Monday
1st ♍
☽ v/c 5:01 am
☽ enters ♎ 7:44 am
Color: Silver

Labor Day

2 Tuesday
1st ♎
Color: Gray

Ramadan begins
Celtic Tree Month of Vine begins
Birthday of Reverend Paul
Beyerl, Wiccan author

3 Wednesday
1st ♎
☽ v/c 1:09 pm
☽ enters ♏ 4:02 pm
Color: Brown

4 Thursday
1st ♏
Color: Turquoise

No man is free who is not a master of himself

5 Friday
1st ♏
☽ v/c 11:45 am
Color: Pink

The Chalice

Chalice, hold all things inside:
Rain and river, tears and tide

Let them splash, a liquid hymn,
Filling you up to the brim

Catch the silver of the Moon
To enchant a Witch's rune

Well of wisdom, dearly sought
Crystal clear the visions brought

Kiss of power, cup of grace
Pour your blessings on this place
                    —Elizabeth Barrette

6 Saturday

1st ♏
☽ enters ♐ 3:11 am
Color: Blue

◑ Sunday

1st ♐
2nd quarter 10:04 am
Color: Amber

It will not matter what spiritual path you are
on if you don't feel it within your being

September

8 Monday

2nd ♐
♃ D 12:16 am
☽ v/c 12:43 pm
☽ enters ♑ 3:45 pm
♇ D 11:14 pm
Color: Ivory

Founding of the Theosophical
Society by H. P. Blavatsky, Henry
Steele Olcott, and others, 1875

9 Tuesday

2nd ♑
Color: Maroon

10 Wednesday

2nd ♑
☽ v/c 9:15 am
♆ ℞ 7:47 pm
Color: Topaz

Birthday of Carl Llewellyn
Weschcke, owner and president
of Llewellyn Worldwide

11 Thursday

2nd ♑
☽ enters ♒ 3:19 am
Color: White

Birthday of Silver RavenWolf,
Wiccan author

12 Friday

2nd ♒
Color: Rose

Nothing evil may pass a circle of fire

Set in Eastern Daylight Time (EDT)

Autumn Equinox Stew

1 T. olive oil
1 onion, diced
3 cloves garlic, minced
1 large eggplant, cubed
1 small acorn squash, peeled, cubed
1 large zucchini, peeled and cubed
1 tsp. salt
black pepper to taste
1 sprig of fresh thyme
3 large tomatoes, diced
1½ cups of water
1 cup of dried lentils

Give thanks for the earth's bounty with this luscious stew made from fresh seasonal vegetables. This stew cooks quickly and can easily be prepared over a festive fire or on the stove.

Put olive oil in a large pot on medium heat. Sauté onion and garlic until highly aromatic. Add eggplant and squash and zucchini. Sauté until edges show signs of cooking. Add remaining ingredients and simmer on medium to low heat for 10 to 15 minutes. Serve with fresh-baked bread or scones.

—Dallas Jennifer Cobb

13 Saturday

2nd ♒
☽ v/c 9:19 am
☽ enters ♓ 12:04 pm
Color: Gray

14 Sunday

2nd ♓
Color: Orange

Phillip IV of France draws up
the order for the arrest of
the French Templars, 1306
Birthday of Henry Cornelius Agrippa,
scholar and magician, 1486

September

☺ Monday
2nd ♓
Full Moon 5:13 am
☽ v/c 3:03 pm
☽ enters ♈ 5:39 pm
Color: Lavender

Harvest Moon

16 Tuesday
3rd ♈
Color: Black

17 Wednesday
3rd ♈
☽ v/c 6:26 pm
☽ enters ♉ 8:56 pm
Color: Yellow

Bewitched debuts on ABC-TV, 1964

18 Thursday
3rd ♉
Color: Purple

19 Friday
3rd ♉
☽ v/c 6:51 pm
☽ enters ♊ 11:17 pm
Color: White

*Agate jewelry can be an inexpensive means of giving
your children protective amulets, especially when they
are going through those clumsy growth spurts*

Set in Eastern Daylight Time (EDT)

Harvest Moon (in Pisces)

The Full Moon in September is often called the Harvest Moon. In agricultural communities, the extra light of the few days around the Full Moon was used to bring in the crops. If the weather is mild, this is a good time for an outdoor Full Moon ritual.

If you can, organize a Harvest Moon picnic with a few friends. Most of the food should be from your gardens, or locally grown, bought at a farmer's market or roadside stand. Traditional foods might be corn, apples, tomatoes, squash, and various greens. Bake your own bread, or try to find a bakery that makes artisan breads. Buy locally made wine or beer.

Find a pleasant place to set up your picnic, a local park or nature preserve, or even a large backyard. Cover a picnic table with a large table-cloth or an old sheet. Arrange the food on the cloth, with ornamental squash, ears of corn, and pumpkins as decorations.

Start the feast by thanking the gods for the bounty of the harvest. After you eat, you can sing, a time-honored way to celebrate. Harvest songs are part of traditional folk music. End with a song of thanks.

—Magenta Griffith

20 Saturday

3rd ♏
Color: Indigo

Camphor trees are sacred in Shinto beliefs, in part
due to their incredible longevity; one camphor tree at
a Shinto shrine is over 1,300 years old

21 Sunday

3rd ♊
Color: Yellow

September

☽ Monday
3rd ♊
4th quarter 1:04 am
☽ v/c 1:04 am
☽ enters ♋ 1:48 am
☉ enters ♎ 11:44 am
Color: Gray

Mabon/Fall Equinox
Sun enters Libra

23 Tuesday
4th ♋
☽ v/c 5:16 pm
♀ enters ♏ 10:59 pm
Color: White

*Kunzite is good for getting rid of emotional
baggage and mending the heart chakra,
as are malachite, emerald, and tourmaline*

24 Wednesday
4th ♋
☿ ℞ 3:17 am
☽ enters ♌ 5:13 am
Color: Brown

25 Thursday
4th ♌
Color: Green

U.S. Senate passes an amendment (705)
attached by Senator Jesse Helms to House
Resolution 3036 (1986 budget bill),
denying tax-exempt status to any organization
that espouses satanism or witchcraft, 1985

26 Friday
4th ♌
☽ v/c 7:20 am
☽ enters ♍ 9:52 am
Color: Purple

Joan Wiliford hanged at Faversham,
England, 1645; she testified that
the Devil came to her in the form of a
black dog that she called "Bunnie"

Set in Eastern Daylight Time (EDT)

Mabon

In agrarian times, the solar event known as Mabon was regarded as a harvest festival to prepare the second round of crops for the looming winter months—a time to complete the harvest that began at Lammas. In terms of the cycle of day and night, Mabon represents sunset, as the Sun retreats and night begins to dominate. Accordingly, contemporary Witches decorate their altars with autumn leaves, pine cones, and acorns along with nuts and dried fruits as offerings to the goddess. As a time of balance, make time for introspection. Reflect on your deeds and celebrate your achievements as the proverbial "fruits of your labor." Think about initiating closure on issues or tasks that are taking a long time to complete, or removing things that no longer serve a purpose.

Traditionally, Mabon is a time to ease the transition from warmth and abundance to the harshness of winter. Whilst the weather is still mild, wash and air your warmer bedding to prepare for ultimate comfort in the weeks ahead. Do the same for your favorite coats and sweaters. You will feel totally organized and ready for the cooler, yet cozy, part of the year!

—Emely Flak

27 Saturday
4th ♍
Color: Blue

28 Sunday
4th ♍
☽ v/c 1:31 pm
☽ enters ♎ 4:05 pm
Color: Gold

Happy is the bride that the Sun shines on
(Irish saying)

September/October

 Monday

4th ♎

New Moon 4:12 am

Color: Silver

---

30 Tuesday

1st ♎

☽ v/c 9:47 pm

Color: Red

Rosh Hashanah

Celtic Tree Month of Ivy begins

---

1 Wednesday

1st ♎

☽ enters ♏ 12:26 am

Color: Brown

Birthday of Isaac Bonewits,
Druid, magician, and Witch

Birthday of Annie Besant,
Theosophical Society president, 1847

---

2 Thursday

1st ♏

☽ v/c 6:46 pm

Color: Green

Ramadan ends

Birthday of Timothy Roderick,
Wiccan author

---

3 Friday

1st ♏

☽ enters ♐ 11:14 am

Color: Purple

Set in Eastern Daylight Time (EDT)

Watchtower of the West

West lies wonder,
Beyond the world's edge
Where the silvering sea
Spills into twilight.
Here the soul sees itself
Deep in the dark water,
A place of reflection and
Parenthood. Dolphins play
With autumn leaves,
Following the ebb tide.
            —Elizabeth Barrette

4 Saturday

1st ♐
♂ enters ♏ 12:34 am
Color: Gray

President Ronald Reagan signs JR 165
making 1983 "The Year of the Bible"
(public law #9728Q); the law states that the
Bible is the word of God and urges a return to
"traditional" Christian values, 1982

5 Sunday

1st ♐
☽ v/c 9:08 pm
☽ enters ♑ 11:48 pm
Color: Gold

October

6 Monday
1st ♑
Color: Lavender

Some rosemary under your pillow
will help you recall your dreams

◐ Tuesday
1st ♑
2nd quarter 5:04 am
☽ v/c 3:37 pm
Color: Maroon

Birthday of Arnold Crowther, stage
magician and Gardnerian Witch, 1909

8 Wednesday
2nd ♑
☽ enters ♒ 12:03 pm
Color: White

9 Thursday
2nd ♒
Color: Purple

Yom Kippur

10 Friday
2nd ♒
☽ v/c 7:13 pm
☽ enters ♓ 9:31 pm
Color: Pink

Set in Eastern Daylight Time (EDT)

11 Saturday
2nd ♓
Color: Brown

The Egyptian god Ra was originally
a sky god, with one eye on the Moon
and the other eye on the Sun

12 Sunday
2nd ♓
Color: Amber

Birthday of Aleister Crowley, 1875

October

13 Monday

2nd ♓
☽ v/c 1:02 am
☽ enters ♈ 3:07 am
Color: Ivory

Columbus Day (observed)

Jacques de Molay and other
French Templars arrested by
order of King Phillip IV, 1306

☺ Tuesday

2nd ♈
Full Moon 4:02 pm
Color: Black

Sukkot begins
Blood Moon

15 Wednesday

3rd ♈
☽ v/c 3:36 am
☽ enters ♉ 5:31 am
☿ D 4:06 pm
Color: Topaz

16 Thursday

3rd ♉
Color: White

*If your child is having disturbing nightmares, try
giving him or her some lapis lazuli to tuck under the pillow*

17 Friday

3rd ♉
☽ v/c 3:33 am
☽ enters ♊ 6:25 am
Color: Rose

Aries Moon

This Aries Full Moon, with the excellent final aspect of Moon trine Pluto, is the best time in months to start something new. Time to consecrate that new tarot deck or wand, to begin a new magical practice, to start a coven. Aries is about action, and Pluto is the mystical planet.

Develop yourself on a material plane as well. Start that exercise program or finally sign up for that class. Seize that opportunity. Starting now will give you an excellent chance to change your life.

A short ritual for new beginnings is simple. Have salt, water, and a red or orange candle handy. Clearly fix your intentions in your mind—if there is a physical object involved in what you are starting, like a registration form for a class, bring it into your ritual. Cast a circle, and light the candle, stating your intention. Then combine salt and water, and use this to bless yourself and the object of your new practice. If it can be damaged by water (like a book), you may use incense instead. Finally, concentrate on the candle, willing a successful outcome, then blow out the candle and close the circle. Keep the candle, and repeat this ritual as your new project continues.

—Magenta Griffith

18 Saturday

3rd ♊
♀ enters ♐ 2:31 pm
Color: Black

Birthday of Nicholas Culpeper,
astrologer and herbalist, 1616

19 Sunday

3rd ♊
☽ v/c 5:52 am
☽ enters ♋ 7:40 am
Color: Orange

The great baobab tree
represents safety in many African societies

October

20 Monday
3rd ♋
Color: Silver

Sukkot ends
Birthday of Selena Fox, Circle Sanctuary

☾ Tuesday
3rd ♋
☽ v/c 7:54 am
4th quarter 7:54 am
☽ enters ♌ 10:35 am
Color: White

22 Wednesday
4th ♌
☉ enters ♏ 9:08 pm
Color: Yellow

Sun enters Scorpio

23 Thursday
4th ♌
☽ v/c 1:53 pm
☽ enters ♍ 3:40 pm
Color: Crimson

*Dreams of crystals and gems indicate you need to find
a more spiritual solution to your problems, or perhaps
you're going to come across some valuable treasure*

24 Friday
4th ♍
Color: White

Samhain Spiders

1½ cups brown sugar
¼ cup soymilk or cow's milk
¾ cup cocoa powder
2 cups rolled oats
1 cup shredded coconut
½ cup chopped nuts (optional)
1 tsp. of vanilla
1 tsp. of margarine or butter

Use a medium saucepan on medium heat. Combine sugar, milk, and cocoa and bring to a boil while stirring continuously. Remove from heat, mix in oats, coconut, nuts (if you want them), vanilla, and butter. Drop onto wax paper using a tablespoon. Cool in fridge or freezer.

Honor the dying season with these deep dark treats. As you melt the ingredients think of the heat of the season past. Combine the other ingredients and meditate on what you want to compost and transform for next year's crops. As you place the spiders into the cooling area, realize that we now move into the dying time.

—Dallas Jennifer Cobb

---

25 Saturday
4th ♍
♂ D 4:13 am
☽ v/c 9:02 pm
☽ enters ♎ 10:47 pm
Color: Blue

Jacques de Molay first interrogated
after Templar arrest, 1306

---

26 Sunday
4th ♎
♀ ℞ 1:55 am
Color: Yellow

De Molay and thirty-one other Templars
confess to heresy in front of an assembly of
clergy; all later recant their confessions, 1306
Sybil Leek dies of cancer, 1982

October/November

27 Monday
4th ♎
Color: Gray

Circle Sanctuary founded, 1974

🌑 Tuesday
4th ♎
☽ v/c 6:05 am
☽ enters ♏ 7:47 am
New Moon 7:14 pm
Color: Red

Celtic Tree Month of Reed begins

29 Wednesday
1st ♏
Color: Brown

MacGregor Mathers issues manifesto
calling himself supreme leader of
the Golden Dawn; all members had to
sign an oath of fealty to him, 1896

Birthday of Frater Zarathustra, who
founded the Temple of Truth in 1972

30 Thursday
1st ♏
☽ v/c 1:45 am
☽ enters ♐ 6:41 pm
Color: Turquoise

House-Senate conferees drop the Senate
provision barring the IRS from granting
tax-exempt status to groups that promote
satanism or witchcraft, 1985

PACT (Pagan Awareness Coalition for
Teens) established in Omaha, Nebraska, 2001

31 Friday
1st ♐
Color: Coral

Samhain/Halloween

Martin Luther nails his ninety-five theses
to the door of Wittenburg Castle Church,
igniting the Protestant revolution, 1517

Covenant of the Goddess founded, 1975

Set in Eastern Daylight Time (EDT)

Samhain

It is believed that the spirits of the dead remain wandering until Samhain, when they can finally cross to the "other side" to rest, as the passage between the living and underworld is open. With this doorway between worlds slightly ajar, the festival of Samhain is also regarded and respected as a time that allows mischievous and restless spirits to make a temporary return to our world.

On this night, take a symbolic journey to the underworld with a virtual or actual walk in a labyrinth. The mystical labyrinth is believed to be a metaphor for the journey of death and rebirth as you travel through the spiral patterns to the core and return on the same path. If you can visit a labyrinth, take the journey. Or you can mark out a temporary labyrinth on sand, or on the ground with twigs, string, or tape. As you travel to the center, leave behind thoughts and images that no longer serve you, shedding unnecessary emotional burdens. Upon reaching the center, stop and imagine you have arrived at the underworld where you can communicate with loved ones who have died. On your walk out, focus on the release and rebirth and enjoy the symbolic transformation.

—Emely Flak

1 Saturday
1st ♐
✳ enters ♑ 8:46 pm
Color: Indigo

All Saints' Day
Aquarian Tabernacle Church established in
the United States, 1979

2 Sunday
1st ♐
♆ D 1:38 am
☽ v/c 4:41 am
☽ enters ♑ 6:13 am
Color: Yellow

Daylight Saving Time ends at 2 am
Circle Sanctuary purchases land
for nature preserve, 1983

November

3 Monday
1st ♑
♀ enters ♍ 12:22 pm
Color: Silver

A necklace or bracelet of amber beads,
when worn, will keep a child healthy

4 Tuesday
1st ♑
☽ v/c 1:47 am
☿ enters ♏ 11:00 am
☽ enters ♒ 7:01 pm
Color: Maroon

Election Day (general)

◐ Wednesday
1st ♒
2nd quarter 11:03 pm
Color: Topaz

6 Thursday
2nd ♒
Color: Green

7 Friday
2nd ♒
☽ v/c 4:33 am
☽ enters ♓ 5:43 am
Color: White

Samhain crossquarter day
(Sun reaches 15° Scorpio)

Set in Eastern Standard Time (EST)

8 Saturday

2nd ♓
Color: Brown

Sentencing of Witches in
Basque Zugarramurdi trial, 1610

Marriage of Patricia and Arnold Crowther
officiated by Gerald Gardner, 1960

9 Sunday

2nd ♓
☽ v/c 11:28 am
☽ enters ♈ 12:26 pm
Color: Orange

Patricia and Arnold Crowther
married in civil ceremony, 1960

November

10 Monday
2nd ♈
Color: Ivory

11 Tuesday
2nd ♈
☽ v/c 2:17 pm
☽ enters ♉ 3:05 pm
Color: White

Veterans Day

12 Wednesday
2nd ♉
♀ enters ♑ 10:25 am
Color: Yellow

A sharkstooth necklace protects the wearer and brings prosperity

☺ Thursday
2nd ♉
Full Moon 1:17 am
☽ v/c 12:12 pm
☽ enters ♊ 3:11 pm
Color: Crimson

Mourning Moon

14 Friday
3rd ♊
Color: Rose

Taurus Moon

The Taurus Full Moon is excellent for material plane works, though the final aspect of Moon opposite Mars makes doing direct work difficult. So be clever: rather than plan the ritual directly, use opposites. Don't state your purpose as, "I want more money," say, "I want poverty in my life to disappear." Better yet, if you can identify barriers that have impeded your progress, work to banish that. For this reason, this Moon also bodes well for some types of healing, especially if you want to get rid of something specific—like acne or excess weight.

Candle magic can be effective for this type of spell. Find a small candle to represent the obstacle in your life. A birthday candle will work well. Be sure to put it in a fireproof holder or container. Compose a short chant, like "Acne vanish," "Obesity away," or "Poverty be gone."

Cast a circle, light the candle, and chant your chant. Visualize the obstacle going away for as long as it takes the candle to completely burn out. When the flame finally flickers and dies, immediately shout, "So mote it be!" and end the circle.

—Magenta Griffith

15 Saturday

3rd ♊
☽ v/c 2:17 pm
☽ enters ♋ 2:52 pm
Color: Blue

Aquarian Tabernacle Church
established in Canada, 1993

16 Sunday

3rd ♋
♂ enters ♐ 3:26 am
Color: Amber

Night of Hecate

November

17 Monday
3rd ♋
☽ v/c 8:43 am
☽ enters ♌ 4:07 pm
Color: Lavender

Birthday of Israel Regardie, occultist
and member of the OTO, 1907

18 Tuesday
3rd ♌
Color: Red

Aleister Crowley initiated into the
Golden Dawn as Frater Perdurabo, 1898

☽ Wednesday
3rd ♌
4th quarter 4:31 pm
☽ v/c 7:48 pm
☽ enters ♍ 8:12 pm
Color: White

Birthday of Theodore
Parker Mills, Wiccan elder, 1924

20 Thursday
4th ♍
Color: Turquoise

Church of All Worlds
incorporates in Australia, 1992

21 Friday
4th ♍
☉ enters ♐ 5:44 pm
Color: Pink

Sun enters Sagittarius

Set in Eastern Standard Time (EST)

The Pentacle

A pentacle is smooth and round
And helps all energies to ground

Its five-point star within a ring
Gives strength and health to everything

Its nature steady as a rock,
Creates for magic's key, a lock

And whether made of stone or clay,
Keeps negativity at bay

For all things fell and fierce are barred
From where a pentacle stands guard
                    —Elizabeth Barrette

22 Saturday

4th ♍
☽ v/c 3:02 am
☽ enters ♎ 3:20 am
Color: Black

23 Sunday

4th ♎
☿ enters ♐ 2:09 am
Color: Gold

Birthday of Lady Tamara Von Forslun,
founder of the Church of Wicca and the
Aquarian Tabernacle Church in Australia

November

24 Monday
4th ♎︎
☽ v/c 12:45 pm
☽ enters ♏︎ 12:54 pm
Color: White

25 Tuesday
4th ♏︎
Color: Gray

Celtic Tree Month of Elder begins
Dr. John Dee notes Edward
Kelley's death in his diary, 1595

26 Wednesday
4th ♏︎
☽ v/c 7:32 am
♇ enters ♑︎ 8:03 pm
Color: Yellow

The mind is not a vessel to be filled,
but a fire to be kindled

☽ Thursday
4th ♏︎
☽ enters ♐︎ 12:14 am
♅ D 11:08 am
New Moon 11:54 am
Color: Green

Thanksgiving Day

28 Friday
1st ♐︎
☽ v/c 7:53 pm
Color: Purple

29 Saturday

1st ♐
☽ enters ♑ 12:48 pm
Color: Blue

30 Sunday

1st ♑
Color: Yellow

Birthday of Oberon Zell,
Church of All Worlds

Father Urbain Grandier imprisoned in
France for bewitching nuns, 1633

December

1 Monday

1st ♑
☽ v/c 10:44 am
Color: Lavender

Birthday of Anodea Judith,
president, Church of All Worlds

2 Tuesday

1st ♑
☽ enters ♒ 1:44 am
Color: Gray

*The basadona is an Italian fairy who rides the
daily breezes, stealing kisses as he goes*

3 Wednesday

1st ♒
☽ v/c 9:14 pm
Color: Brown

4 Thursday

1st ♒
☽ enters ♓ 1:23 pm
Color: Green

*Goddess imagery in a dream often
represents female strength and confidence*

○ Friday

1st ♓
⚸ enters ♈ 12:01 am
2nd quarter 4:25 pm
Color: White

Pope Innocent VIII reverses the
Canon Episcopi by issuing the bull
Summis Desiderantes Affectibus, removing
obstacles to Inquisitors, 1484
Death of Aleister Crowley, 1947

The Crone Goddess

The Crone sits in Her rocking chair
And roasts the chestnuts on the coals.
Outside, December branches bear
A coat of frost in curling scrolls.

She frightens children with Her eyes
And thumps Her cane, a solemn beat –
But ah, Her words are gentle, wise,
A waning crescent at Her feet.

Her death draws near; She knows it's so,
But does not fear what it will bring
For underneath the fallen snow,
The tulip bulbs are dreaming spring.
                        —Elizabeth Barrette

---

6 Saturday

2nd ♓
☽ v/c 7:43 pm
☽ enters ♈ 9:44 pm
Color: Indigo

Death of Jacob Sprenger, coauthor
of the *Malleus Maleficarum*, 1495

Birthday of Dion Fortune, member
of the Golden Dawn, 1890

---

7 Sunday

2nd ♈
♀ enters ♒ 6:36 pm
Color: Amber

In Russian folklore, the bear is the friend of
humankind, capable of giving sound advice

December

8 Monday
2nd ♈
☽ v/c 4:35 pm
Color: White

9 Tuesday
2nd ♈
☽ enters ♉ 1:52 am
Color: Maroon

*Imagination is the only weapon
in the war against reality*

10 Wednesday
2nd ♉
☽ v/c 5:23 pm
Color: Yellow

*A sprig of St. John's wort over the doorway
will protect a child from evil*

11 Thursday
2nd ♉
☽ enters ♊ 2:33 am
Color: Turquoise

☺ Friday
2nd ♊
☿ enters ♑ 5:12 am
Full Moon 11:37 am
☽ v/c 1:01 pm
Color: Pink

Long Nights Moon

Set in Eastern Standard Time (EST)

Gemini Moon

The Full Moon in Gemini is excellent for divination, rituals to seek inspiration, or brainstorming. You could incorporate all three by using bibliomancy. Take a book about the subject you wish to explore. Open it at random and, without looking, point on the page. Read the sentence your finger landed on. Does that passage give you any new ideas or insights? Repeat three or four times, either with the same book, or different books on the same subject. Meditate on the sentences you have read.

Another way to seek ideas is to invoke the Muses. The nine daughters of Zeus and Mnemosyne were each attributed to a different art: epic and heroic poetry, music, lyric and erotic poetry, history, tragedy, sacred poetry and geometry, dance, comedy, and astronomy and astrology.

Choose the Muse most relevant to your field. Prepare an altar with symbols of your art or other specialty. Include a picture of the Muses, or your Muse, if you can. Cast a circle, then ask for help and inspiration. Promise to pursue your art faithfully. Do some artistic work, spend a little time in circle writing, drawing, singing, or practicing your instrument.

—Magenta Griffith

13 Saturday

3rd ♊
☽ enters ♋ 1:39 am
Color: Blue

First papal bull against black magic
issued by Alexander IV, 1258

14 Sunday

3rd ♋
☽ v/c 5:27 pm
Color: Orange

December

15 Monday
3rd ♋

☽ enters ♌ 1:22 am
⚷ D 11:33 pm
Color: Gray

16 Tuesday
3rd ♌

☽ v/c 7:45 pm
Color: Red

*Tawny agate is prized in Persia and Italy for its
ability to protect against the evil eye*

17 Wednesday
3rd ♌

☽ enters ♍ 3:35 am
Color: Topaz

*To guard against magic,
wear a golden bracelet set with topaz on your left arm*

18 Thursday
3rd ♍

Color: Crimson

*Early Christians believed that the Holy Grail was
encrusted with pearls, providing it with magical properties*

☽ Friday
3rd ♍
☽ v/c 5:29 am
4th quarter 5:29 am
☽ enters ♎ 9:23 am
Color: Purple

128   *Set in Eastern Standard Time (EST)*

Yule

At Yule, the Oak King who rules during the waxing year conquers the Holly King in order to reign until Midsummer, when the two meet again. It is believed that the Holly King has evolved into the modern day Santa Claus, wearing red, with holly in his hat. His eight deer represent the Pagan sabbats, as animals are regarded sacred by the Celtic gods. Although the Oak King and the Holly King are opposing forces at Litha and Yule, they comple-

ment each other. In ancient times, the Sun's return after a long period of scarcity and darkness affirmed survival and resilience in the winter season.

A few days before Yule, decorate your home with oranges studded with cloves to release a warm, yuletide aroma. It's a time to feast, exchange gifts, and thank the Goddess for the return of abundance and light. At your Yule gathering, cozy up to your favorite people and enjoy some delicious mulled red wine infused with cinnamon sticks and whole cloves. Serve warm in chalices, with a sprinkle of nutmeg, to toast the rebirth of the Oak King. When you take a sip from the chalice, hold hands with your guests and shout, "Wassail"—the old English word for "your health."

—Emely Flak

20 Saturday

4th ♎
Color: Black

21 Sunday

4th ♎
☉ enters ♑ 7:04 am
☽ v/c 11:57 am
☽ enters ♏ 6:36 pm
Color: Gold

Yule/Winter Solstice
Sun enters Capricorn
Janet and Stewart Farrar begin
their first coven together, 1970

December

22 Monday
4th ♏︎
Color: Silver

Hanukkah begins

23 Tuesday
4th ♏︎
Color: Black

24 Wednesday
4th ♏︎
☽ v/c 12:29 am
☽ enters ♐︎ 6:13 am
Color: White

Christmas Eve
Celtic Tree Month of Birch begins

25 Thursday
4th ♐︎
Color: Purple

Christmas Day
Feast of Frau Holle, Germanic weather goddess
who was believed to travel through
the world to watch people's deeds;
she blessed the good and punished the bad

26 Friday
4th ♐︎
☽ v/c 6:25 pm
☽ enters ♑︎ 6:56 pm
Color: Coral

Kwanzaa begins
Dr. Fian arraigned for twenty counts
of witchcraft and treason, 1590

Set in Eastern Standard Time (EST)

Yule Cranberry Cookies

2¼ cups flour (spelt also works)
¾ cups sugar
1 tsp. baking soda
½ tsp. salt
½ tsp. cinnamon
⅓ cup soymilk or cow's milk
¼ cup olive oil
½ cup margarine or butter
¼ cup of silken tofu or 2 eggs
1 cup of cranberries—fresh or frozen
½ cup sunflower seed
¾ cup of almonds chopped

Heat the oven to 350 degrees F. Mix all the dry ingredients in a large bowl. Add soymilk, margarine or butter, olive oil, tofu or eggs, and mix well. Add cranberries, sunflower seeds, and almonds and mix well. Use a tablespoon to put globs on the nonstick cookie sheet. Press flatter with a fork. Bake for 10 to 12 minutes or until golden brown.

Let these golden orbs remind—the germination of the seed deep beneath the surface begins now as the solar cycle shifts toward the light. Celebrate the day with bright foods and people. Light candles, feast, and call forth the Sun.

—Dallas Jennifer Cobb

☽ Saturday
4th ♑
♂ enters ♑ 2:30 am
⚷ enters ♉ 4:47 am
New Moon 7:22 am
Color: Indigo

Birthday of Gerina Dunwich,
Wiccan author

28 Sunday
1st ♑
Color: Yellow

December/January

29 Monday

1st ♑
☽ v/c 4:20 am
☽ enters ♒ 7:42 am
Color: Ivory

Hanukkah ends
Islamic New Year

30 Tuesday

1st ♒
Color: White

For all sad words of tongue and pen,
the saddest are these, "It might have been"
—John Greenleaf Whittier

31 Wednesday

1st ♒
♄ ℞ 1:08 pm
☽ v/c 1:34 pm
☽ enters ♓ 7:27 pm
Color: Topaz

New Year's Eve
Castle of Countess Bathory of Hungary
raided, 1610; accused of practicing black
magic, she murdered scores of the local
townsfolk; she was walled up in a room in
her castle, where she later died

1 Thursday

1st ♓
☿ enters ♒ 4:51 am
Color: Purple

New Year's Day
Kwanzaa ends

2 Friday

1st ♓
Color: Coral

Watchtower of the North

North stand the mountains,
A wall of old women and men,
Heads hoary with snow.
Bulls bellow in the high meadows.
The winds of winter roar,
But stone stands fast.
The body bears its burdens,
A warm home for the soul.
Starlight fills the dark, cold night.
Stand fast. Stand firm. Forever.
　　　　—Elizabeth Barrette

3 Saturday
1st ♓
☽ v/c 3:50 am
☽ enters ♈ 4:50 am
♀ enters ♓ 7:35 am
Color: Indigo

4 Sunday
1st ♈
2nd quarter 6:56 am
☽ v/c 9:44 pm
Color: Orange

About the Authors

ELIZABETH BARRETTE, the managing editor of *PanGaia*, has been involved with the Pagan community for more than eighteen years, and has done much networking with area Pagans including coffeehouse meetings and open sabbats. Her other writing includes speculative fiction and gender studies. In 2005, her poem "The Poltergeist of Polaris" earned a nomination for the Rhysling Award. She lives in central Illinois and enjoys herbal landscaping and gardening for wildlife.

DALLAS JENNIFER COBB lives in an enchanted waterfront village. When not scheming novel ways to pay the bills, she's running country roads or wandering a beach. Her essays are in recent Seal Press anthologies *Three Ring Circus* and *Far From Home*. Her video documentary *Disparate Places* appeared on TV Ontario's *Planet Parent*. Contact this regular contributor to Llewellyn's almanacs at Jennifer.Cobb@Sympatico.ca.

ELLEN DUGAN, the "Garden Witch," is a psychic-clairvoyant and a practicing Witch of twenty years. Ellen is a Master Gardener and teaches classes on flower folklore and gardening at a community college. She is the author of several Llewellyn books including: *Garden Witchery*, *Elements of Witchcraft*, *7 Days of Magic*, *The Enchanted Cat*, *Herb Magic for Beginners*, and *Natural Witchery*. Ellen and her family live in Missouri.

GERINA DUNWICH is a priestess of the Old Religion, a paranormal investigator, astrologer, and the author of more than two dozen books on witchcraft, the paranormal, and the occult arts. She is the founder of the Paranormal Animal Research Group, the Pagan Poets Society, and the

Bast-Wicca tradition. She lives in upstate New York and is the proprietress of an antique shop that also sells metaphysical books and occult supplies.

EMELY FLAK is a practicing solitary Witch from Daylesford, Australia. When she is not writing, she is at her "day job" as a learning and development professional. Recently, this busy mother of two and partner of one completed training to be a civil celebrant. Much of her work is dedicated to embracing the ancient wisdom of Wicca for personal empowerment.

MAGENTA GRIFFITH has been a Witch for nearly thirty years and is a founding member of the coven Prodea, which has celebrated rituals since 1980. She has been a member of the Covenant of the Goddess, the Covenant of Unitarian Universalist Pagans, and Church of All Worlds. She presents workshops and classes at festivals around the Midwest.

JENNIFER HEWITSON has been a freelance illustrator since 1985. Her illustrations have appeared in local and national publications including the Wall Street Journal, the Washington Post, the Los Angeles Times, US News & World Report, and Ladybug magazine. Her advertising and packaging clients include Disney and the San Diego Zoo. Jennifer has created a line of greeting cards for Sun Rise Publications, and has illustrated several children's books. Her work has been recognized by numerous organizations, including the Society of Illustrators Los Angeles, and magazines such as Communication Arts, Print, and How.

DIANA RAJCHEL lives, works, worships, and writes in Minneapolis, Minnesota. She is the organizer of the Twin Cities Urban Magic Project and also assists in the planning of Twin Cities Pagan Pride. Sometimes she works with organizations that need assistance in the care and feeding of volunteers. You can learn more about her at www.dianarajchel.com.

LAUREL REUFNER, a solitary Pagan for over a decade, is active in the Circle of Gaia Dreaming and the CUUPS chapter near her southeastern Ohio home, which she shares with her husband and two daughters.

K. D. SPITZER is an experienced astrologer, teacher, and writer living on the seacoast of New Hampshire, where she is always assigned the Hecate role in ritual. Known for her legendary honey cakes, Ms. Spitzer also publishes and edits The Country Wisdom Almanac, an uncomplicated compendium designed to bring the power of the planets to daily life.

ABBY WILLOWROOT is the founder of the Goddess 2000 Project, the Spiral Goddess Grove, and Willowroot Real Magic Wands. A full-time professional Goddess artist, wand maker, and writer since 1965, her work has appeared in many metaphysical publications. Nine pieces of Ms. Willowroot's jewelry are in the Smithsonian Institution's permanent collection.

Appendix

Daily Magical Influences

Each day is ruled by a planet with specific magical influences.

Monday (Moon): peace, healing, caring, psychic awareness
Tuesday (Mars): passion, courage, aggression, protection
Wednesday (Mercury): study, travel, divination, wisdom
Thursday (Jupiter): expansion, money, prosperity, generosity
Friday (Venus): love, friendship, reconciliation, beauty
Saturday (Saturn): longevity, endings, homes
Sunday (Sun): healing, spirituality, success, strength, protection

Color Correspondences

Colors are associated with each day, according to planetary influence.

Monday: gray, lavender, white, silver, ivory
Tuesday: red, white, black, gray, maroon, scarlet
Wednesday: yellow, brown, white, topaz
Thursday: green, turquoise, white, purple, crimson
Friday: white, pink, rose, purple, coral
Saturday: brown, gray, blue, indigo, black
Sunday: yellow, orange, gold, amber

Lunar Phases

Waxing, from New Moon to Full Moon, is the ideal time to do magic to draw things to you.

Waning, from Full Moon to New Moon, is a time for study, meditation, and magical work designed to banish harmful energies.

The Moon's Sign

The Moon continuously moves through each sign of the zodiac, from Aries to Pisces, staying about two and a half days in each sign. The Moon influences the sign it inhabits, creating different energies that affect our day-to-day lives.

Aries: Good for starting things. Things occur rapidly, but quickly pass. People tend to be argumentative and assertive.

Taurus: Things begun now last longest, tend to increase in value, and become hard to change. Brings out an appreciation for beauty and sensory experience.

Gemini: Things begun now are easily changed by outside influence. Time for shortcuts, communication, games, and fun.

Cancer: Stimulates emotional rapport between people. Supports growth and nurturing. Tend to domestic concerns.

Leo: Draws emphasis to the self, to central ideas or institutions, away from connections with others and emotional needs.

Virgo: Favors accomplishment of details and commands from higher up. Focus on health, hygiene, and daily schedules.

Libra: Favors cooperation, compromise, social activities, balance, friendship, and partnership.

Scorpio: Increases awareness of psychic power. Precipitates psychic crises and ends connections thoroughly. People have a tendency to brood and become secretive.

Sagittarius: Encourages confidence and flights of imagination. This is an adventurous, philosophical, and athletic Moon sign. Favors expansion and growth.

Capricorn: Develops strong structure. Focus on traditions, responsibilities, and obligations. A good time to set boundaries and rules.

Aquarius: Rebellious energy. Time to break habits and make abrupt change. Personal freedom and individuality is the focus.

Pisces: The focus is on dreaming, nostalgia, intuition, and psychic impressions. A good time for spiritual or philanthropic activities.

2008 Eclipses

February 6, 10:56 pm; Solar eclipse 17° ≈ 44'
February 20, 10:27 pm; Lunar eclipse 1° ♍ 53'
August 1, 6:22 am; Solar eclipse 9° ♌ 32'
August 16, 5:11 pm; Lunar eclipse 24° ≈ 21'

2008 Full Moons

Cold Moon: January 22, 8:35 am
Quickening Moon: February 20, 10:30 pm
Storm Moon: March 21, 2:40 pm
Wind Moon: April 20, 6:25 am
Flower Moon: May 19, 10:11 pm
Strong Sun Moon: June 18, 1:30 pm
Blessing Moon: July 18, 3:59 am
Corn Moon: August 16, 5:16 pm
Harvest Moon: September 15, 5:13 am
Blood Moon: October 14, 4:02 am
Mourning Moon: November 13, 1:17 am
Long Nights Moon: December 12, 11:37 am

Planetary Retrogrades in 2008

Planet		Date	Time		Direct	Date	Time
Mars	℞	11/15/07	3:24 am	—	Direct	01/30/08	5:33 pm
Saturn	℞	12/19/07	9:09 am	—	Direct	05/02/08	11:07 pm
Mercury	℞	01/28/08	3:31 pm	—	Direct	02/18/08	9:57 pm
Pluto	℞	04/02/08	5:23 am	—	Direct	09/08/08	11:14 pm
Jupiter	℞	05/09/08	8:11 am	—	Direct	09/08/08	12:16 am
Mercury	℞	05/26/08	11:48 am	—	Direct	06/19/08	10:31 am
Neptune	℞	05/26/08	12:14 pm	—	Direct	11/02/08	1:38 am
Uranus	℞	06/26/08	8:01 pm	—	Direct	11/27/08	11:08 am
Mercury	℞	09/24/08	3:17 am	—	Direct	10/15/08	4:06 pm
Saturn	℞	12/31/08	1:08 pm	—	Direct	05/16/09	10:06 pm

Set in Eastern Time. All times corrected for Daylight Saving Time.

Moon Void-of-Course Data for 2008

Last Aspect		New Sign	
Date	Time	Sign	New Time

JANUARY

Date	Time	Sign	New Time
1	7:33 pm	♏	8:32 pm
3	7:30 pm	♐	9:13 am
6	7:27 pm	♑	8:43 am
8	6:37 am	♒	6:13 am
11	12:52 pm	♓	1:44 pm
13	6:41 pm	♈	7:23 pm
15	10:39 pm	♉	11:13 pm
17	9:05 pm	♊	1:30 am
20	2:46 am	♋	3:05 am
21	5:56 pm	♌	5:20 am
24	9:43 am	♍	9:48 am
26	6:32 am	♎	5:35 pm
28	4:47 pm	♏	4:35 am
31	3:34 am	♐	5:08 pm

FEBRUARY

Date	Time	Sign	New Time
2	5:21 pm	♑	4:52 am
4	1:20 pm	♒	2:10 pm
7	10:50 am	♓	8:46 pm
9	4:05 pm	♈	1:17 am
11	8:00 pm	♉	4:34 am
14	12:05 am	♊	7:19 am
16	5:17 am	♋	10:12 am
17	4:13 pm	♌	1:51 pm
20	12:52 pm	♍	7:06 pm
22	9:14 pm	♎	2:44 am
25	8:35 am	♏	1:05 pm
27	9:53 am	♐	1:22 am

MARCH

Date	Time	Sign	New Time
1	11:54 am	♑	1:33 pm
3	1:16 am	♒	11:24 pm
5	4:46 pm	♓	5:53 am
7	2:04 pm	♈	9:23 am
10	7:09 am	♉	12:13 pm
12	1:26 pm	♊	1:54 pm
14	4:23 pm	♋	4:37 pm
16	2:58 pm	♌	9:04 pm
18	2:38 pm	♍	3:25 am
20	3:28 pm	♎	11:45 am
23	8:41 am	♏	10:06 pm
25	8:36 pm	♐	10:11 am
28	9:21 am	♑	10:43 pm
31	12:54 am	♒	9:34 am

APRIL

Date	Time	Sign	New Time
2	5:13 am	♈	4:55 pm
4	5:43 pm	♉	8:27 pm
6	11:01 am	♊	9:19 pm
8	11:12 am	♋	9:27 pm
10	12:11 pm	♌	10:43 pm
12	2:32 pm	♍	2:29 am
15	12:56 am	♎	9:06 am
17	1:59 pm	♏	6:10 pm
19	4:54 pm	♐	5:00 am
22	4:53 am	♑	5:07 pm
24	5:37 pm	♒	5:47 am
27	10:18 am	♓	5:27 pm
30	1:25 am	♈	2:11 am

MAY

Date	Time	Sign	New Time
2	5:34 am	♈	6:51 am
4	3:16 am	♉	7:58 am
6	4:21 am	♊	7:17 am
7	9:36 pm	♋	7:02 am
9	8:06 pm	♌	9:10 am
12	4:09 am	♍	2:48 pm
14	12:38 pm	♎	11:46 pm
16	11:29 pm	♏	10:59 am
19	10:11 pm	♐	11:18 pm
22	12:19 am	♑	11:55 am
24	8:26 am	♒	11:51 pm
26	10:49 pm	♓	9:38 am
29	2:23 am	♈	3:52 pm
31	8:54 am	♉	6:18 pm

JUNE

Date	Time	Sign	New Time
2	9:02 am	♊	6:06 pm
4	8:08 am	♋	5:16 pm
6	5:32 am	♌	6:00 pm
8	11:40 am	♍	10:01 pm
10	3:42 pm	♎	5:55 am
13	5:15 am	♏	4:53 pm
15	5:29 pm	♐	5:19 am
18	5:37 pm	♑	5:51 pm
20	3:02 pm	♒	5:33 am
23	3:04 pm	♓	3:32 pm
25	10:16 pm	♈	10:49 pm
28	2:14 pm	♉	2:50 am
30	2:43 am	♊	4:03 am

JULY

Date	Time	Sign	New Time
2	3:08 am	♋	3:53 am
3	4:13 pm	♌	4:15 am
6	6:04 am	♍	7:04 am
8	12:21 pm	♎	1:31 pm
10	10:14 pm	♏	11:35 pm
12	11:05 pm	♐	11:50 am
15	10:44 pm	♑	12:20 am
18	3:59 am	♒	11:40 am
20	7:25 pm	♓	9:07 pm
23	2:39 am	♈	4:22 am
25	7:30 am	♉	9:14 am
27	12:52 am	♊	11:55 am
29	11:25 am	♋	1:11 pm
31	1:31 am	♌	2:21 pm

AUGUST

Date	Time	Sign	New Time
2	2:59 pm	♍	4:59 pm
4	8:16 pm	♎	10:28 pm
7	5:01 am	♏	7:26 am
9	5:02 pm	♐	7:10 pm
12	5:04 am	♑	7:42 am
14	1:09 pm	♒	6:56 pm
17	1:14 am	♓	3:46 am
19	7:41 am	♈	10:10 am
21	12:53 pm	♉	2:38 pm
23	5:19 am	♊	5:48 pm
25	5:52 pm	♋	8:18 pm
27	8:13 pm	♌	10:51 pm
29	11:44 pm	♍	2:18 am

SEPTEMBER

Date	Time	Sign	New Time
1	5:01 am	♎	7:44 am
3	1:09 pm	♏	4:02 pm
5	11:45 am	♐	3:11 am
8	12:43 pm	♑	3:45 pm
10	9:15 am	♒	3:19 am
13	9:19 am	♓	12:04 pm
15	3:03 pm	♈	5:39 pm
17	6:26 pm	♉	8:56 pm
19	6:51 pm	♊	11:17 pm
22	1:04 am	♋	1:48 am
23	5:16 pm	♌	5:13 am
26	7:20 am	♍	9:52 am
28	1:31 pm	♎	4:05 pm
30	9:47 pm	10/1 ♏	12:26 am

OCTOBER

Date	Time	Sign	New Time
9/30	9:47 pm	1 ♏	12:26 am
2	6:46 pm	♐	11:14 am
5	9:08 pm	♑	11:48 pm
7	3:37 pm	♒	12:03 pm
10	7:13 pm	♓	9:31 pm
13	1:02 am	♈	3:07 am
15	3:36 am	♉	5:31 am
17	3:33 am	♊	6:25 am
19	5:52 am	♋	7:40 am
21	7:54 am	♌	10:35 am
23	1:53 pm	♍	3:40 pm
25	9:02 pm	♎	10:47 pm
28	6:05 am	♏	7:47 am
30	1:45 am	♐	6:41 pm

NOVEMBER

Date	Time	Sign	New Time
2	4:41 am	♑	6:13 am
4	1:47 am	♒	7:01 pm
7	4:33 am	♓	5:43 am
9	11:28 am	♈	12:26 pm
11	2:17 pm	♉	3:05 pm
13	12:12 pm	♊	3:11 pm
15	2:17 pm	♋	2:52 pm
17	8:43 am	♌	4:07 pm
19	7:48 pm	♍	8:12 pm
22	3:40 am	♎	3:20 am
24	12:45 pm	♏	12:54 pm
26	7:32 am	♐	12:14 am
28	7:53 pm	♑	12:48 pm

DECEMBER

Date	Time	Sign	New Time
1	10:44 am	♒	1:44 am
3	9:14 pm	♓	1:23 pm
6	7:43 pm	♈	9:44 pm
8	4:35 pm	♉	1:52 am
10	5:23 pm	♊	2:33 am
12	1:01 pm	♋	1:39 am
14	5:27 pm	♌	1:22 am
16	7:45 pm	♍	3:35 am
19	5:29 am	♎	9:23 am
21	11:57 am	♏	6:36 pm
24	12:29 am	♐	6:13 am
26	6:25 pm	♑	6:56 pm
29	4:20 am	♒	7:42 am
31	1:34 pm	♓	7:27 pm

Set in Eastern Time. All times corrected for Daylight Saving Time.

Name:

Address, City, State, Zip:

Home Phone: Office Phone:

E-mail: Birthday:

Name:

Address, City, State, Zip:

Home Phone: Office Phone:

E-mail: Birthday:

Name:

Address, City, State, Zip:

Home Phone: Office Phone:

E-mail: Birthday:

Name:

Address, City, State, Zip:

Home Phone: Office Phone:

E-mail: Birthday:

Name:

Address, City, State, Zip:

Home Phone: Office Phone:

E-mail: Birthday:

Name:

Address, City, State, Zip:

Home Phone: Office Phone:

E-mail: Birthday:

Name:

Address, City, State, Zip:

Home Phone: Office Phone:

E-mail: Birthday:

Name:

Address, City, State, Zip:

Home Phone: Office Phone:

E-mail: Birthday:

Name:

Address, City, State, Zip:

Home Phone: Office Phone:

E-mail: Birthday:

Name:

Address, City, State, Zip:

Home Phone: Office Phone:

E-mail: Birthday:

Name:

Address, City, State, Zip:

Home Phone: Office Phone:

E-mail: Birthday:

Name:

Address, City, State, Zip:

Home Phone: Office Phone:

E-mail: Birthday:

Name:

Address, City, State, Zip:

Home Phone: Office Phone:

E-mail: Birthday:

Name:

Address, City, State, Zip:

Home Phone: Office Phone:

E-mail: Birthday:

Name:

Address, City, State, Zip:

Home Phone: Office Phone:

E-mail: Birthday:

Name:

Address, City, State, Zip:

Home Phone: Office Phone:

E-mail: Birthday:

Name:

Address, City, State, Zip:

Home Phone: Office Phone:

E-mail: Birthday:

Name:

Address, City, State, Zip:

Home Phone: Office Phone:

E-mail: Birthday:

Name:

Address, City, State, Zip:

Home Phone: Office Phone:

E-mail: Birthday:

Name:

Address, City, State, Zip:

Home Phone: Office Phone:

E-mail: Birthday:

Name:

Address, City, State, Zip:

Home Phone: Office Phone:

E-mail: Birthday:

Name:

Address, City, State, Zip:

Home Phone: Office Phone:

E-mail: Birthday:

Name:

Address, City, State, Zip:

Home Phone: Office Phone:

E-mail: Birthday:

Name:

Address, City, State, Zip:

Home Phone: Office Phone:

E-mail: Birthday:

Name:

Address, City, State, Zip:

Home Phone: Office Phone:

E-mail: Birthday:

Name:

Address, City, State, Zip:

Home Phone: Office Phone:

E-mail: Birthday:

Name:

Address, City, State, Zip:

Home Phone: Office Phone:

E-mail: Birthday:

Name:

Address, City, State, Zip:

Home Phone: Office Phone:

E-mail: Birthday:

Name:

Address, City, State, Zip:

Home Phone: Office Phone:

E-mail: Birthday:

Name:

Address, City, State, Zip:

Home Phone: Office Phone:

E-mail: Birthday: